I0650481

Job Scott

The Baptism of Christ

A Gospel Ordinance - Being Altogether Inward and Spiritual

Job Scott

The Baptism of Christ
A Gospel Ordinance - Being Altogether Inward and Spiritual

ISBN/EAN: 9783743393264

Manufactured in Europe, USA, Canada, Australia, Japa

Cover: Foto ©Lupo / pixelio.de

Manufactured and distributed by brebook publishing software (www.brebook.com)

Job Scott

The Baptism of Christ

THE

BAPTISM OF CHRIST,

A

GOSPEL ORDINANCE:

BEING ALTOGETHER

INWARD AND SPIRITUAL:

Not, like John's, into Water; but, according to the real nature of the
Gospel, into the very name, life, and power of the FATHER, and of
the SON, and of the HOLY GHOST.

Shewing that the Apostles' use of Water Baptism was by no means as an
Ordinance of CHRIST, but as the Baptism of John; and that all who
are baptized into CHRIST, have put on CHRIST, not only professionally
but substantially—that is, have put him on as the whole Armour of
Light, and walk in him in newness of Life.

―――――――――

By *J. O B S C O T T.*

―――――――――

PROVIDENCE, PRINTED:

L O N D O N,

REPRINTED BY JAMES PHILLIPS, GEORGE-YARD,

LOMBARD-STREET.

1794.

PREFACE.

THIS little treatife, reader, is written chiefly for the help and information of fuch as are in a ftate of honeft enquiry, and who have not yet feen clearly beyond fome of thofe former obfervances, which at the very beft were but preparatory, and pointing to him, and his work on the foul, in whom they all end, and are done away forever; but partly for the confirmation and eftablifhment of fuch as have been already convinced of the unfhadowy difpenfation of the gofpel.

I HAVE long feen with forrow, that many fincere fouls are much detained from the fubftance, by undue attachments to the fign. I have once known and groaned under this bondage and entanglement myfelf; for though I was never a partaker in any of thofe outward ordinances, yet I was divers years blinded in my underftanding, through the vail that was over me, in reading the accounts of baptifm in the New Teftament. I could not underftand why the Apoftles ufed water, efpecially after Chrift's refurrection, if it was not Chrift's baptifm; nor how men could poffibly baptize with the Holy Ghoft; and therefore finding men commanded to baptize, and that they did baptize with water, I concluded, very ignorantly, that water was commanded by Chrift. —This conclufion, I have fince feen, was the natural refult of inexperience, in an anxious in-

veftigation

veſtigation of things not known by mere human
wiſdom, or creaturely abilities, but only ſpirit-
ually diſcerned; and as my mind was ſincerely
engaged to ſee for myſelf, and avoid all decep-
tion, it pleaſed him who has the key of David,
(after I had paſſed ſeveral years of doubt and he-
ſitation, ſometimes concluding I ſhould before
long be baptized in water, and then ſtruck with
an inward and feeling conviction of its utter in-
ſufficiency towards effecting the renovation and
cleanſing which my ſoul at times longed for) to
open my underſtanding, chiefly by his own internal operations and illuminations in my enquiring
mind, without much of any inſtrumental means,
either reading or hearing; ſo that I ſaw clearly,
(which I had too long been very dull in believing, and fearful in receiving) that Chriſt himſelf
in ſpirit had long time been ſtriving with me,
moving in me, wooing, calling, knocking, check-
ing, reſtraining, conſtraining, and powerfully im-
preſſing my mind; but I knew him not, and in that
inward and immediate way ſought not after him.
When, alas! had I but known the gift of God,
and who it was that inwardly talked with me,
I might have aſked of him, and received the
living water of his heavenly kingdom; as afterwards I did, to the full ſatisfaction of my thirſty
ſoul.   And when this became my joyful experience, wherein the beloved of my ſoul met with me,
as with many others, in the garden, ſaying "eat,
O friends—drink, yea drink abundantly, O
beloved," Cant. v. 1, I became perfectly ſatisfied,
that outward bread, wine and water, were no part
of the baptiſm or ſupper of the Lord, nor any
way neceſſary to his anointed, in things pertain-
-ing to ſalvation.   It was not very long after this,

                                            before

before I not only believed, but knew, by moft
confolatory experience, that men, even in our
day, though helplefs of themfelves, are through
divine affiftance enabled iuftrumentally, in a very
powerful and heart-watering manner, to baptize
with the Holy Ghoft. For being now engaged to
feel after God, if happily I might from time to
time renewedly find him, he was not only pleafed
in thefe my filent approaches, in religious meet-
ings, and more retired waitings, to arife in me immediately, with the brightnefs of a morning without clouds, and powerfully to manifeft himfelf to
me and in me, as a fountain of living waters; but
was alfo gracioufly pleafed to fend among us, of
his fervants, fuch as were well qualified to do the
work of evangelifts, and who being largely acquainted with the foul-faving baptifm of Chrift
in themfelves, were fo filled with the Holy Ghoft,
and fpake fo demonftratively, in the life, evidence,
and divine virtue and vigour of it, that it was like
the oil poured on Aaron's head, which ran down
to the very fkirts of his garment—it even reached,
overflowed, and filled my poor foul.

Much I could write refpecting thefe bleffed
days of my efpoufals, but enlargement here may
be improper; I fhall therefore juft fay, that had I
not felt living defires that others may come to a
full participation of the fame bleffed experience,
and that none may be longer unprofitably amufed
and detained, by lifelefs figns and fymbols, from
the all-fufficient fubftance, thou, reader, had never heard from me in this way.—I know many
find their intereft in keeping up a fhow in thefe
things, and reprefenting them of exceeding great
importance.—I have no doubt many very fincerely

urge

urge them upon their friends and acquaintance, as believing them injunctions of the gospel; but I am also sadly sensible that too many "seek their gain from their quarter," and obtain it, by keeping up a lifeless round of prayers, preaching, singing, eating, drinking, dipping, sprinkling, &c. and am convinced beyond scruple, that the mammon of unrighteousness, this way increased, is a powerful obstruction to the coming of the kingdom of our Lord, in life and power, unclouded and uneclipsed by the retention of vailing and darkening observances.—Babylon is not yet so fallen, as to rise no more : she is still lurking in a mystery.—She is still mystery Babylon the great, and still the mother of many harlots—thousands are ensnared among some or other of her daughters, and are not aware of her cup.—May the Lord graciously preserve the honest-hearted, of every denomination, from the harmful influences of all her many and artful sorceries, and keep alive their hunger and thirst after true righteousness.— I have no doubt but that, if I am finally so happy as to reign in life by Jesus Christ, my only hope and Saviour, I shall be there accompanied by thousands, who have through their whole lives lived under the vail, as to outward ordinances; but who, having in great sincerity done what they believed was their duty, in singleness as unto God, and not unto men, are and finally will be well accepted of him, who seeth not as man seeth, but looks through all outside things to the heart. And yet, on the contrary, I do firmly believe many, who have began and ran well for a season, have been by degrees, as outward things have become more and more considerable with them, drawn more and more from the true hunger, and.

been

been more and more eafy and fatisfied with little
or nothing of the true bread, water and wine, of
the kingdom, till at length they have centered in
formality, and fat down in a reft fhort of the foul's
falvation.—That thou mayeft fhun this dangerous
rock, dear reader, and be preferved living and
growing in the holy root of divine life, to the end
of thy ftay here, and finally admitted to the joys
of the bleffed, forever to adore and blefs the God
of all grace and true confolation, is the prayer of
thy fincere friend, and willing fervant in the labour and travail of the gofpel,

THE AUTHOR.

The Baptism of CHRIST, a Gospel Ordinance, &c.

CHAP. I.

Of the regular order and succession of divine dispensations. Signs and figures pointed at life and substance. Hence Christ deferred his gospel ministry, till John's course in a baptism, but figurative of his own, was fulfilled. John's baptism and Christ's are type and antitype. Christ sent his disciples to baptize with his own baptism. So breathes on them the Holy Ghost. Great wisdom even in the timing our Lord's baptism by John, also in his answer to John. John preached the kingdom but at hand. In its nature and fulness, it is after, not before, nor joined with the type. John prepared the way. Some took the kingdom by force. All types end in the antitype. Christ's baptism cleanses thoroughly, as John's was total immersion. A picture, as truly a man, as water baptism Christ's. A single eye, all of light, and then the shadow is behind us. Christ was baptized in water, not to continue, but fulfil that decreasing sign; and so to make way for the increasing substance. He also ate, and thus fulfilled the passover.

IT is very observable, that our Lord Jesus Christ deferred the open and express promulgation of the gospel of the kingdom till John the Baptist, his immediate forerunner, had fulfilled his course; and that not before, but after John had finished his prepatory ministration, ceased
the

the voice crying in the wildernefs, prepare, &c, quite ended his own decreafing work in that outward elementary baptifm, which as a fign was to precede and prepare the way for Chrift's, and was fhut up in prifon; he, the Lord of life and glory, the end and ender of all typical difpenfations, immediately entered upon the publication of the gofpel word; the new, the increafing and ever continuing difpenfation of life, fubftance and falvation.—For we read, Mat. iv. 12, " now when Jefus had heard that John was caft into prifon, he departed into Galilee." And verfe 17, " from that time Jefus began to preach, and to fay, repent; for the kingdom of heaven is at hand." This kingdom, now fo near at hand, and which John had juft before proclaimed to be fo, was and is inward and fpiritual; for our Lord himfelf declares, " the kingdom of God is within you," Luke xvii. 21. And it is clear that he waited for John's courfe to be firft fulfilled, before he ever began publicly to preach it. See alfo Mark i. 14. 15. " Now after that John was put in prifon, Jefus came into Galilee, preaching the gofpel of the kingdom of God; and faying, the time is fulfilled, and the kingdom of God is at hand; repent ye, and believe the gofpel." The gofpel is not fign or figure, but life and fubftance, the " power of God to falvation," free from all types and fhadows, being the laft and lafting difpenfation; and which was not to commence in its general fulnefs, till after all others. Chrift is often fpoken of as coming after John; and John, as going, or coming, or being fent before Chrift: and therefore as John's courfe in the very laft of the fhadows, water baptifm, was now completed, the great minifter of the fanctuary very

pertinently,

pertinently, at the very beginning of his own gofpel preaching, proclaimed, the time is fulfilled.
I know not what words he could have ufed more
proper and fignificant to introduce the glorious
gofpel, and teach mankind that all figns were to
end in the fubftance. And from a fincere wifh for
the real good and folid information of mankind,
I defire this one word, fulfilled, in this and divers
other places, may be fpecially noticed, and deeply
confidered. It is of vaft importance.

AND why did Jefus wait till John's courfe was
fulfilled? why, then, immediately on hearing of
his imprifonment, did he begin to preach the gofpel of the kingdom as then juft at hand? and why
was he fo careful, at his very entrance on this
great work, to make this fpecial declaration, " the
time is fulfilled? There is deep inftruction in it
all. He knew the times and feafons, though
many who could difcern the face of the fky, and
had underftanding in the forebodings of change
in regard to the weather, were and are ignorant of the figns of the times; and through
this ignorance many did, and many ftill do, retain
the fhadow out of all proper feafon. But Chrift,
as he knew, fo he carefully obferved the right
time. He would have all things pertaining to
his kingdom, efpecially his own immediate tranf-
actions, take place in their proper feafons. He
would not haften his firft great miracle in Cana,
of turning water into wine, even though his own
mother folicitoufly prompted him to that glorious exertion of his divinity.—He would not go
up to the feaft, till the right time. So neither
would he begin his own public miniftration (which
was for the ending of all fhadows, the abolition
                                                    and

and blotting out the hand-writing of ordinances)
till John's (which was much in the shadow) was
fulfilled. " The law and the prophets prophesied
until John." John was himself both a prophet
and under the law, yet he and his miniftration were
until Chrift. His coming after the reft of the
prophets, being fent immediately before the face
of the Lord, and to prepare his way, in no wife
hindered his being a prophet himfelf. Chrift teftifies, among them that are born of women, there
hath not rifen a greater, Mat. xi. 11. He alfo fays,
Mat. v. 17, 18, " think not that I am come to
deftroy the law or the prophets ; I am not come
to deftroy, but to fulfil ; for verily I fay unto
you, till heaven and earth pafs, one jot or one
tittle fhall in no wife pafs from the law, till all be
fulfilled." Here we fee he came to fulfil both
the law, and the predictions of the prophets. Accordingly we read of divers things faid to be done,
that it might be fulfilled which was fpoken by the
prophets, or fpoken aforetime. Hence, though
John came after the others, and as it were reached from them to Chrift, yet he too came under
the law, and was one among the prophets, which
Chrift came not to deftroy, but whofe predictions and forerunning difpenfations he came to
fulfil. John's prophetic declaration was eminently
pertinent, in regard to the great work of Chrift in
gofpel baptifm, the fanctification of fouls ; and fo
was his figurative immerfion : and Chrift, in his
faving baptifm, amply fulfils both the prophecy
and the fign. Chrift was " made under the law"
himfelf, Gal. iv. 4; then furely fo was John.
And feeing John's watery miniftration was to
prepare Chrift's way, and lead to his faving baptifm ; Chrift having thus carefully deferred his
own

own public miniftration till John's was fulfilled, as foon as this was done, and John caft into prifon, the right time being now exactly arrived, he went forthwith, on hearing of John's imprifonment, into Galilee; and there and " from that time began to preach," and proclaim the word and gofpel of that unfhadowy difpenfation and kingdom, which ends and fulfils all mere figns and figures and is to increafe and remain of perpetual continuance. Hence Peter declares the word " was publifhed throughout all Judea, and began from Galilee, after the baptifm which John preached," Acts x. 37; and may we not fafely conclude, from Peter's fo particularly mentioning this, as being after John's baptifm, and from the evangelift's mentioning it as after his imprifonment, that they had heard our Lord exprefs his acting on fpecial principle in thus deferring his own public miniftry, till his forerunner's, in that forerunning baptifm, was fulfilled; and efpecially as his going into Galilee, to begin his faid public miniftry, is exprefsly faid to be, " that it might be fulfilled which was fpoken by Efaias the prophet ?" Mat. iv. 14.

THUS it feems he acted with fpecial defign, both as to the place where and the time when he began the open publication of the glorious gofpel. It was therefore with divine pertinency, that as he began this gracious publication, he firft of all announced " the time is fulfilled." His hour was now come. For well knowing when it was and when it " was not yet come," he had now waited till John had firft preached, according to Paul's teftimony, " the baptifm of repentance to all the people of Ifrael;" and fo had "fulfilled his courfe."
See

See Acts xiii. 24, 25. All this tends forcibly and beautifully to open both the necessity of his being baptized of John just then when he was, and the meaning of his answer, when John forbade him. John knew his own baptism was not saving, was not Chrift's; but was to decreafe and end in Chrift's, being only defigned for our Lord's manifeftation to Ifrael, and to prepare the people for his faving baptifm.—And knowing this, John plainly and honeftly teftifies, that he fhould be made manifeft to Ifrael, " therefore am I come baptizing with water," John i. 31. This plain and full teftimony, from the mouth of John himfelf, at once evinces that his baptifm, being but with water, was far different from Chrift's, and inferior to it; and that it was to introduce, or as a fign to affift in turning the minds of the people to look for, receive and fubmit to the burning, purifying baptifm of the gofpel.—In fhort, water baptifm and Chrift's are plainly type and antitype ; and accordingly Peter, fpeaking of the baptifm which now faves, ufes the Greek word antitypon, 1 Pet. iii. 21.

Peter doubtlefs knew the type or figure could not fave. It is " the ingrafted word which is able to fave" the foul, James i, 21. Chrift fanctifies and cleanfes the church " with the wafhing of water by the word." Eph. v. 26. This " ingrafted word," this fanctifying " wafhing of water by the word," is all inward and fpiritual. It is the antitype of the divers wafhings under Mofes, and equally fo of water baptifm, in every form. This cleanfes the foul, as outward water does the body, and puts away the filth of the fpirit, as that does the filth of the flefh. Hence, and hence only,

only, it is faving: herein is the alone propriety
of Peter's words, "baptifm doth alfo now fave
us." As Chrift came to fulfil the law of commandments, contained in outward ordinances,
and to end every difpenfation of figns and
fhadows, he had many things to fubmit to, on
purpofe to fulfil the typical righteoufnefs of
thofe difpenfations. Hence he was circumcifed,
kept the law, celebrated the paffover, &c. On
the fame ground, it behoved him to be baptized
in water, the laft lively typical reprefentation of
his own great work of fanctification, that is, the
laft in the courfe of time preceding his beginning
the publication of the gofpel word from Galilee.
But when he came to John to be baptized of him,
John not knowing his defign in it, nor why it muft
be fo, forbade him, faying, "I have need to be
baptized of thee, and comeft thou to me?" Mat.
iii. 14. It is not at all ftrange that John forbade
him; for he knew his own baptifm, being outward, typical, and preparatory, was to decreafe
and give place to Chrift's. It was "unto repentance;" by a total outfide immerfion, it pointed
out the neceffity of the removal of all fin, and
bringing "forth fruits meet for repentance." It
was ufed for his manifeftation to Ifrael, whofe fiery
baptifm alone could effect this inward cleanfing
fiom all fin. Chrift was neither ignorant of himfelf, nor guilty of fin. Hence he could not receive
John's figurative immerfion upon the fame grounds
as others did, neither in order to repentance and
remiffion of fin, nor in order to be made manifeft
to himfelf. John doubtlefs marvelled, therefore,
to fee him come to his baptifm. For though it
feems he did not, before this, fo fully know him to
be the Chrift as he did afterwards, yet on his now

coming

coming to him, it feems he had fome fenfe and knowledge of it, and marvelled at his coming. But our Lord gracioufly condefcended to fhow on what grounds it was now neceffary: that it was neither in order to repentance in him, nor to a manifeftation of him to himfelf, nor yet to perpetuate a fymbolical inftitution under the gofpel; but, on the contrary, to fulfil it. Chrift knew the fign muft precede the fubftance. He knew the many fymbols of the law were but "a fhadow of things to come," Col. ii. 17; that the law, with all its figurative offerings, cleanfings, and divers wafhings, was a fchool-mafter for a feafon, to lead to himfelf, the fubftance; fee Gal. iii. 24. He knew "the baptifm which John preached" was the peculiar fign or reprefentation of his own, and was ufed to prepare the people's minds for it, and thereby prepare in their hearts the way of the Lord, and lead forward to his faving manifeftation to Ifrael. Therefore had he began the publication of the gofpel of that fpiritual kingdom, which is without figns and fhadows, and cometh not with outward obfervation, before John, the adminiftrator of a baptifm figurative thereof, had firft fulfilled his courfe in that figurative adminiftration, it would by no means fo fully, ftrikingly and inftruftively have anfwered and illuftrated the defigns of eternal wifdom, as his deferring it till afterwards; for, how then could John's work have been ftriftly according to God's defign in fending him? that is, to prepare the way of the Lord—to go before him—and make ready a people prepared for him; fee Luke i. 17.

HENCE it was neceffary, that in the courfe of God's divine Providence, and divers difpenfations,

tions, he who has to go before our Lord in the power and spirit of Elias, thus to prepare his way, should be sent seasonably to begin and " fulfil his course," in that ministration and baptism which was in order to the manifestation of the great gospel baptizer, before the publication of that word which began from Galilee, after his baptism. Hence also it was necessary that Jesus should be baptized in the figure, and thus accomplish what he had to do outwardly in the fulfilment of water baptism, previously to that wonderful descent of the Holy Ghost upon him. For as he was to be " anointed to preach the gospel" (see Luke iv. 18.) and as this anointing was by the Spirit of the Lord that was upon him, and not by his baptism in water, therefore, as the time drew near that he must enter, thus anointed, upon his public ministry, it behoved him first to submit to John's baptism, that all things might be done in proper season, and follow in regular succession, one after another.

THE Almighty had given John beforehand to understand, that he on whom he should see the Holy Ghost not only descending, but also remaining on him, " the same is he which baptizeth with the Holy Ghost," John i. 33. Thus was the descent and abiding of the Holy Ghost, even on our Lord himself, pointed out as that which alone could qualify to baptize others with it; and it will hold good of all his disciples and ministers to the world's end. Therefore they have his promise to be with them by his Spirit, the Holy Ghost, in the execution of his great commission, to baptize into the divine name and power of Father, Son, &c. And as all sent by him to baptize with the

B   Holy

Holy Ghoſt muſt be firſt ſo baptized themſelves, he ſat the glorious example. And when he came afterwards to ſend them forth in the great work of baptizing, he declared with divine propriety, " as my Father hath ſent me, even ſo ſend I you." And ſhewing plainly how that was, he " breathed on them, and ſaith unto them, receive ye the Holy Ghoſt," John xx. 21, 22. See how exactly he ſent them to baptize, &c. as his Father ſent him. His Father, ſending him to baptize with the Holy Ghoſt, breathed it, or cauſed it to deſcend and abide upon him. This proved and proclaimed him to be the baptizer with it; he ſending his ſervants to baptize with the ſame baptiſm, breathed on them, that they might receive a meaſure of the qualification as he received of his Father. And this was truly neceſſary —the ſame work requires the ſame qualifications —" he that believeth on me," (ſays Chriſt) " the works that I do, ſhall he do alſo," John xiv. 12.

He was not baptized with water, to qualify him ſo to baptize others; for he baptized none in water; the work which he did in baptiſm, was inward, and with the Holy Ghoſt—the ſpiritual purifying fire of the Lord. He did not breathe on his diſciples, and baptize them with the Holy Ghoſt, to qualify them to baptize others in water; that had not been ſending them, as his Father ſent him: it had not been ſending them, nor enabling them to do the ſame work, and baptize with the ſame baptiſm, as he did. Had he, after breathing on them, ſent them, qualified with the Holy Ghoſt, to baptize with a mere element, it had been very different from his Father's ſending him in the

the power and baptifm of the Holy Ghoft, to
baptize others with the fame. And as their qualification to adminifter his spiritual baptifm was
that of the Holy Ghoft coming upon them; fo,
in his own cafe, the defcent and abiding thereof
upon him was the very thing made ufe of by the
wifdom of God, whereby to manifeft him more
clearly unto John, as the gofpel baptizer. Seeing,
therefore, this his qualification for baptizing with
his own great gofpel baptifm, which is after and
fuperior to all figns, muft be received from on
high, before he began that glorious gofpel miniftry, which is alfo without figns, it was, as before
noted, neceffary for him previoufly to fubmit to that baptifm, which being but a fign,
was to decreafe and end in the fubftance, which
the fign pointed to.—Hence the neceffity of his
waiting till John had firft baptized many of the
people, borne teftimony to one coming after him,
and turned their minds to the neceffity of his
more fpiritual and refining baptifm.—And hence
alfo the neceffity of his receiving that baptifm
which was only in the fign, and to vanifh as the
fubftance was experienced; not after, but before
he received that defcent and abiding of the Holy
Ghoft upon him, which pointed him out as the
great adminiftrator of that baptifm which, in
the very order of things, is after that which
is but a fhadow of the good things to come.
Thus the type was kept in its time and place;
before, not after, the antitype. But had
not Chrift's baptifm in the type, to fulfil
it, as a thing ending in the antitype, been prepof-
terous, had it been after his glorious antitypical
baptifm and anointing, by the defcent and abiding
of the Holy Ghoft upon him?—This being the
cafe, there is evidently a very beautiful difplay of

B 2   wifdom

wifdom and propriety in our Lord's anfwer to
John, when John forbade him. Indeed every
part of it to me, feems full of divine inftruction.
It fatisfied John, and removed all his fcruples ; for
though he did not at firft know that Jefus muft
be baptized as well as circumcifed, in the figure,
and fubmit to the other figurative inftitutions of
the law, in order to fulfil all the figurative or typical righteoufnefs of the feveral difpenfations
preceeding the gofpel ; yet he feems well to have
known that his baptifm muft vanifh and decreafe,
as being in its nature outward, and in its defign
but preparatory to Chrift's. Hence, fays he, " he
muft increafe, but I muft decreafe," John iii. 30.
" I indeed baptize you with water, but he fhall
baptize you with the Hóly Ghoft," verfe 11.
And thus knowing the preparatory, decreafing
and terminating nature and defign of water baptifm, what further he wanted to know, to induce
him to baptize our Lord, was, that in order properly to decreafe and fulfil what he already knew
muft decreafe and be fulfilled, the Lord of life
and glory muft ftoop to it himfelf ; and therefore,
as foon as the bleffed Jefus had convinced him of
this, he readily, without more ado, baptized him.
—And of this our Lord's anfwer at once convinced him, it being full to the purpofe. Let us
trace it.

THE very firft word is inftructive. " Suffer it
to be fo," Mat. iii. 15, as if he had faid—I indeed have no need of it, no fin to repent of—nor
do I wifh it done to manifeft me to myfelf ; it is
not at all of neceffity to me in this fenfe ; thou,
John, art therefore rather to fuffer it, than adminifter it as thou doft to others, to teach them
their

their neceffity of a thorough cleanfing, and turn
their minds to me and my baptifm, which alone
can effect it.—It is true, as thou art fenfible, this
is not my baptifm, nor any part of my gofpel
difpenfation : mine, all have need of: thou art
right in faying thou thyfelf haft need to be baptized of me. And as mine is the alone gofpel baptifm, it is not ftrange that thou admireft at my
fubmitting to that of water; for truly it would be
highly contrary to the purity and fimplicity
of my gofpel, to perpetuate any ceremonial obfervances under the full funfhine thereof; but
this is by no means my intention, but directly the
reverfe; I do it on purpofe to fulfil outfide things,
and make way for me to introduce, and publifh
to the world, that gofpel which is after, and to
end all types and fhadows: and which, for that
very reafon, I cannot properly even begin the
publication of before; but muft, in order to a
regular procedure, defer, till after I have fubmitted to this figurative baptifm which thou
preacheft. By which thou mayeft clearly fee,
that in baptizing me in the figure, a thing fo different from my unfigurative baptifm and gofpel,
thou art properly fpeaking, to fuffer it to be fo.
—Next the word now is ftrikingly fignificant.
"Suffer it to be fo now." This important word
is not ufed here without fpecial propriety and defign—it is the dictate of eternal wifdom; for now
was the very juncture of time, now the pure unfhadowy gofpel difpenfation was but at hand, not
yet brought in. Chrift had not yet fuffered ; nay,
he had not yet even began publicly to promul-
gate the gofpel of that kingdom, the baptifm of
which is only fpiritual; and therefore he might
now properly partake of that which only pointed
to it, and was to end in it. And further, now

was

was the exact period for him to do what he had to
do outwardly in fulfilling it; becaufe John had
now preached the baptifm of repentance to many,
if not literally, as Paul fays, to all the people of
Ifrael, Acts xiii. 24, perhaps to nearly, or quite
all, in thofe parts.—At leaft, according to Mat.
iii. 5, we may conclude, they of Jerufalem, and
all Judea, and all the region round about Jordan,
had now been baptized of John, and Chrift was
now foon to begin his own gofpel miniftry, and
therein to preach the kingdom of heaven, as an
internal unfigurative difpenfation, to the fouls of
men. Now therefore was the very time, in the
course and order of things, for him to be baptized
in outward water; the acceptable moment for
John to fuffer it to be fo. John had, as he
baptized the people, diligently preached the
kingdom at hand, not yet fully come, and
taught them to look beyond his outward, to
Chrift's inward and faving baptifm.—This he
powerfully and pofitively declared fhould be effected by one then among them, though they
knew him not. So near was the kingdom now
at hand, and faft approaching. This greatly
raifed their expectations. Indeed the fire of
Chrift's baptifm began to kindle in fome of
their hearts; for Chrift declares he came to fend
fire on the earth; "and what will I" (fays he)
"if it be already kindled?" Luke xii. 49. It truly
was fo in fome degree in many minds, even
that very fire whereby his baptifm thoroughly
cleanfes, in its complete operation, the whole floor
of the heart. Therefore it was now time for him
foon to begin his public gofpel teftimony, which
in ftrict propriety ought to, and in fact did, fucceed, not precede, the baptifm of water, which
was John's— and by which, and the preaching attending

tending it, John had thus prepared the people for
Chrift's according to the exprefs defign of his
miffion; which was, as noted before, " to make
ready a people prepared for the Lord."

JOHN's preaching, baptifm, and fingular life,
being in the defert till the time of his fhewing
unto Ifrael, then wearing a leathern girdle, and
coat of camels hair, neither eating flefh nor drinking wine, but eating locufts and wild honey, &c.
wrought greatly on the minds of many. They
mufed much of John; and were anxious to know,
whether he were the Chrift or not. John declared honeftly he was not; but that he was vaftly
unworthy, in comparifon of him—that his baptifm was but with water, a very inferior thing,
compared with Chrift's—defigned to prepare for
it, and juft ferving in order to his manifeftation
to Ifrael, and then to decreafe and give place to
him and his baptifm, which is to increafe, and of
the increafe whereof there is no end.—John was
truly modeft, and fought not to defraud Chrift of
any of his glory; but honeftly and openly both
confeffed his own inferiority, and turned the
people's attention from himfelf to his Lord, faying, " Behold the Lamb of God, which taketh
away the fin of the world," John i. 29.—Thus
the time haftened—the ftate of things ripened.
—Indeed the " kingdom of heaven fuffered violence." And the minds of fome, under the pref-
fure of what they felt working in them, rufhed
into it as it were by force; that is, before the full
time for its more glorious and ample difplay and
eftablifhment, which was not to be till Chrift had
fuffered.—Hence, fays Jefus, Mat. xi. 12, " from
the days of John the Baptift, until now, the kingdom of heaven fuffereth violence, and the vio-

lent

lent take it by force." Their hearts were fo engaged, and the working of the feed or leaven of
the kingdom was fo prevalent in them, that, as
it were by a kind of violent anticipation, they
took, or obtained, fome real poffeffion and enjoyment of the pure antitypical life, liberty, power
and fubftance of the fpiritual kingdom of God;
before that more glorious out-breaking, and more
general eftablifhment and exaltation thereof
among the people, which took place after Chrift
had fuffered, and had fulfilled all the fymbolical
righteoufnefs of figns and fhadows, and triumphed
over them all, nailing them to his crofs? thus
afcending up on high, leading captivity captive,
and bountifully giving gifts unto men.

And why is the kingdom faid to fuffer this
kind of violence from the days of John the Baptift, but becaufe the power of his miniftry, his
living teftimony concerning Chrift, and his baptifm had greatly wrought upon their hearts?
John's preaching and defcription of Chrift's baptifm was very awakening—he ftruck againft all
falfe dependencies—nothing would do fhort of
fruits worthy of a ftate of real unfeigned repentance; no claims of outward defcent from Abraham
—nor any mere plungings in water, no partial
cleanfings or half-way reformations; not one or
two only, but every corrupt tree of the whole
heart muft be hewn down, and caft into the fire.
Thus the axe was now laid to the very root of
the tree; lopping the branches only would not
do— it muft come to thorough work, even to
burning up all the chaff, and gathering the wheat,
winnowed therefrom, into the garner of the Lord.
—This doctrine was fo forcibly promulgated by
John, and had fuch effect upon fome who were
                                                    waiting

waiting for the confolation of Ifrael, that it was now time for Jefus to fubmit to John's baptifm, in order to the fulfilment of the typical righteouf-nefs thereof, and to make way for the word, gofpel and antitypical righteoufnefs of his own inward and fpiritual kingdcm among them.—Thus urgent and preffing was the neceffity of our Lord's foon entering upon his own public mini-ftration in the work of the everlafting gofpel, and which he accordingly did enter upon almoft im-mediately after John's imprifonment.—Well there-fore might he, as to his baptifm in water, urge it upon John to " fuffer it to be fo now," juft now, without further delay: for thus it becometh us, fays he, to fulfil all righteoufnefs.—Obferve the word all—for even the moft outward, typical and decreafing inftitutions, that had really been of. God, of right demanded veneration; it was a point of real righteoufnefs rightly to obferve, and rightly to fulfil them. And as Chrift came to " blot out the hand-writing of ordinances, and take it out of the way," (fee Col. ii. 13) and fo to bring his people to a fingle attention to the new covenant written in the heart, and of which he himfelf is mediator; it did truly and highly be-come him, feeing he came not to redeem from the bondage of the law, and rudiments or fhadows of good things, by deftroying; but by fulfilling, to unite with John in fulfilling water baptifm; for that could no more pafs rightly away, till it was fulfilled, than any other outward ordinance. —All the fhadows were but for a time, and to end in the fubftance—and fo faithful was Chrift in all his work and office, that he would not fuffer a jot or tittle to pafs from the law, till all was fulfilled. Hence on the fame ground he

fays

fays to John, "it becometh us to fulfil all righteoufnefs." The righteoufnefs of that ordinance
of water baptifm, was at beft but under or during
the law of outward commandments. Immerfion in
water was enjoined and had often been practifed
among the Jews before, and baptifm was in fome
fort and on fome occafions ufed as an initiatory
ordinance among them. John indeed ufed it
fomewhat differently, but both he himfelf and his
baptifm were previous to the abrogation of the
ceremonial law, which continued in force till
feveral years after he had quite fulfilled his courfe,
even till our Lord's refurrection.

INDEED Jefus himfelf enjoined its punctual obfervance; fo true is the Apoftle's teftimony, that
he was "made under the law," Gal. iv. 4; and
was under tutors and governors till the time appointed of the Father, verfe 2 : fo that the expreffions of the law and Prophets prophecying until
John, are of no more authority to difprove
John's being ftrictly under the law, than they
are to difprove his being ftrictly a prophet.

CHRIST declares him a Prophet, yea and more
than a Prophet. And his being more than a
Prophet, is the true ground of this diftinction refpecting the law and the Prophets prophecying
until John; not that either the law or the Prophets had then ceafed, but John, as great a Prophet as any born of woman, and as truly under
the law, was alfo fo much more than a Prophet,
that he was the immediate forerunner of our
Lord ; a voice proclaiming him not as coming
afar off, but as then ftanding among the people,
or as it were a finger pointing directly to him, as
then

then come in that body of flesh. And it is remarkable, how much John's preaching and testi-
mony concerning Christ are confined to his foul-
purifying baptism. This, and a plain, full and
repeated destination and description of the very
great difference between this and that with water,
seems to be the main scope and subject with John.
And there is much divine wisdom and propriety in
its being so; for John was the only administrator
of water baptism, even specially ordained, and
sent of God, as such. He ran not of himself, as
it is to be feared many now do; God sent him,
yea sent him expresly to baptize with water, according to John i. 33; and why? plainly " that
Christ might be made manifest to Israel," as before noticed.

Now, therefore, as baptism in water was that
peculiar outward action, or ordinance, which was
chosen and directed of God, to prepare the way
of his Son, introduce and manifest him to Israel;
we may depend upon it, it was because he would
have him specially manifested and introduced to
their notice and acceptance, as the great gospel
baptizer, refiner and purifier of souls.—In short,
the baptism of Christ comprehends so much, so
nearly all, in the work of sanctification, and crea-
tion anew in him, that the Father Almighty, in
his unlimited goodness, and good will to men,
took special care that John, the preparer of his
way, in the power and spirit of Elias, should be expresly sent before him, baptizing in water, as a
lively resemblance and representation of his great
work, in thoroughly cleansing the floor of the heart.
This was John's proper business. Hence he is
repeatedly and almost constantly called John
the

the Baptift, or baptizer, as fome tranflate it.
He went before the face of the Lord, (baptizing
men's bodies) to prepare his way as the baptizer
of fouls. For this reafon, he dwells almoft
wholly on the defcription of Chrift's baptifm,
the manner of his effecting it, the operations
and effects of it, and the very great fuperiority of
it to that of water.

In words, he fully and forcibly inculcates, that
in its complete operation it effects an entire
purification—no corrupt or even unfruitful
tree is to be left—nor chaff remaining with the
wheat.—The fire of this baptifm is holy, yea the
fire of the HolyGhoft; and where the heart fubmits
to its influence, it is, fo long as filth remaineth,
truly unquenchable; it burns till all is confumed,
till the drofs, and tin, and, what is more, the reprobate filver (however fpecious in appearance,
and current among many for true devotion, and
real religion) is feparated and done away from
the gold; for the veffels in the Lord's houfe
fpiritually are made of beaten gold, fuch as have
endured the Lord's fire, and been refined in his
furnace; for this only can bear the hammer, fo
as thereby to be beaten and formed into chofen
veffels in his holy houfe, which "holinefs becometh forever." See Pfalm xciii. 5. And as his houfe
is a houfe of holinefs; fo the way of his ranfomed is a "way of holinefs; the unclean fhall not
pafs over it," Ifai. xxxv. 8. None can walk in it
but in proportion as they are baptized with the
Holy Ghoft, and purifying fire, and thus made
fit veffels for the Lord's houfe; for the Prophet
Zachariah, xiv. 21, winds up his prophecy of
gofpel times with a pofitive declaration, that in
                                        that

that day "every pot in Jerufalem and in Judah
fhall be holinefs unto the Lord of Hofts."

THAT this ftate might be attained, we have
feen that John's defcription of Chrift's baptifm,
even to the very inhabitants of Jerufalem and
Judea, outwardly (though I think little of local-
ity in this cafe) reprefents it as effecting thorough purification, as perfecting holinefs in the
fear of the Lord. And this he not only teaches
in words , but fhews them in his manner of baptizing, plunging them all over in water, as if he
would have riveted it in their minds, that nothing
fhort of complete fatisfaction would anfwer.

HE indeed baptized them in water, and even,
in that, though merely a figure of the one gofpel
baptifm, he plainly held forth perfection, or perfect cleanfing, or why did he wafh them all
over? If Chrift's baptifm effects only a partial,
half-way cleanfing in this life, would not a partial,
half-way, wafhing, or fprinkling, more properly
have reprefented it, and therefore have been a
more proper way to have prepared the way of
the Lord, and furthered his manifeftation to
Ifrael ?

SURELY his forerunner ought fo to prepare his
way, as to give a juft idea of him, and of his
work; and fo to reprefent and fhadow out his
baptifm, as to raife proper fentiments and defires
in the well difpofed refpecting it. And this, in
fact, he was very careful to do; for as he was
fo much more than a Prophet, that he was
fpecially appointed, and fent to prepare Chrift's
way, and eminently to contribute, by that very
fignificant figure, towards his proper manifeftation

tion to Ifrael, he fell not behind the reft of the Prophets in teftimony to the fulnefs and completenefs
of that baptifm, whereby Chrift faves his people,
not in but from their fins. He was fo faithful
to his truft, that, not fatisfied with repeated me-
taphorical illuftrations of it by word of mouth,
as of the axe, fan, and fire, yea unquenchable
fire, all centering in one point, that of abfolute
and full purification; he went one ftep further;
he dipped great numbers of them fo totally into
the water, that if they would underftand any
thing by it of the nature and extent of Chrift's
baptifm, they could fcarcely underftand any
thing fhort of what was typically intended by it.
And having thus powerfully prepared the way of
the Lord, by preparing the people to receive him
in the adminiftration of that baptifm which faves
the foul from fin, it was now time for the Lord
himfelf to be baptized, in that very figure by
which his baptifm was thus ftrikingly reprefented; not to perpetuate it, and induce the people to
think more highly of it; but, quite on the
contrary, fo far to fulfil it, as to make way
for that reprefented by it. For thofe outward
obfervances, by which the fubftance was reprefented (as the figure of a man reprefents the
man it is the figure of) were none of them
any more the fubftance itfelf, than the figure
of a man is the man.

Some are very fond of the mere picture, the
lifelefs figure of their dearefts friends, in their
abfence; but few are fo weak as to pay much
regard to the picture, when they are in actual
enjoyment of the prefence, the endearing company, and fweet converfation of their friends.

Water

Water baptifm is not a whit more the baptifm of Chrift, than the figure of a man is
the man. And they who are now baptized
therewith, and eat and drink outward bread
and wine, in remembrance of Chrift, have, in
thefe performances abftractedly, no more of
the real baptifm and fupper of the Lord, than
a man may have of his friend, in the picture
of him. I fay not that a man cannot ufe thefe
things, and at the fame time enjoy fomething
of the fubftance fignified by them. A man
may enjoy fomething of the real and delight-
ful prefence of his friend, and yet have his
picture in the room, and fometimes look at it,
but whenever his attention is fixed clofely upon
the picture, it is infallibly diverted in the fame
proportion from his friend, though then alive
and prefent. And fo it is in thefe figurative
obfervations. In proportion as they are objects
of attention, the mind is diverted from, or
ftops fhort of the thing fignified. And hence
I think it generally holds good, that thofe who
are very tenacious of them, moft zealous in
their ufe, urge them the moft preffingly on others,
and moft liberally cenfure and condemn thofe,
who, believing them to be no gofpel ordinances,
confcientioufly decline them; are lefs livingly
fenfible of the life and fubftance, than fome
others, who, though they alfo ufe them, are far
lefs built up in and tenacious of them. At the
very beft, they are but fhadows of the good
things.—" If thine eye be fingle" (to the light
of Chrift) " thy whole body fhall be full of light."
See Mat. vi. 22. Only keep thine eye fingle,
and fixed upon the outward fun, and the fhadow
will be behind thee, and out of thy fight. Turn

about

about, and fix thine eye full on the shadow,
and then the sun will be behind thee; and whilst
thou art fixed in attention to the shadow, thou
wilt fee little or nothing of the face of the
sun. Thus some who begin in the Spirit, turn
about, and seek to be made perfect in the
flesh, or in outward ordinances. But granting
thy attention not singly to the shadow, yet try it
a thousand ways, and thou shalt never be able
to pay either less or more attention thereto;
but thou wilt be obliged to have thy attention
proportionally less to the sun, than it would
be, wert thou equally attentive, and that
attention singly directed to the sun.—In like
manner, the man whose eye is single to the
divine light of Jesus in his own heart, and
whose attention is steadily to the work of his
baptism there, has as much more true and sub-
stantial experience of the blessed and saving
operation and effects thereof, than the man,
who, equally attentive, suffers his attention to
be divided, and partly diverted to the outward
figures; as a man in close and single attention to
the sun, has more of its light, and sees more of
its real brightness and glory, than he who observes
an equal attention on the whole, but suffers it to
be divided between the sun and the shadow.
—And this I take to be the very ground and
reason of our Lord's faithful fulfilment of all
such figurative righteousness, that so his servants
might press forward to the substance signified,
and figured out thereby. Paul told the Galatians, "if ye be circumcised, Christ shall pro-
fit you nothing," Gal. v. 2. This must amount
to thus much at least, that in proportion as
they relied on, or were taken up with attention

to that outward performance, they were diverted from Chrift—and this is juft as true of
water baptifm, and every other outward fymbol.—I fuppofe many may readily drink it down,
that fo certainly as a man is outwardly circumcifed, he can have no benefit at all from
Chrift, who yet think outward baptifm an ordinance of his gofpel: but what found reafon
can be given, why one outward ordinance,
once abfolutely commanded of God, but now
ceafed in point of obligation, to give place to
the fubftance once fignified by it, fhould fo
much more effectually prevent our being profited by Chrift, than another outward ordinance,
in like manner once commanded of God, but
long fince as fully ceafed in point of obligation, and for the fame reafon, to give place to
the fubftance?

THE truth is, every outward obfervation, whatever, fo far as it diverts the mind from inward
attention to the work of Chrift, fo far it prevents effectually our being profited by him. And
I am forry to perceive fuch numbers of profeffing
Chriftians ftriving fo hard, as I think they do,
to make thefe things ferve as a fubftitute for
that which is faving. They evidently fubftitute
water baptifm inftead of Chrift's; for they do not
fcruple to call it the one baptifm of the gofpel.
They exprefsly maintain it to be Chrift's, and apply
to it many texts which evidently fpeak of far
deeper matters; as baptifm into Chrift, into his
death, &c. and that which fpeaks of the baptifm
which now faves us, although the text itfelf
declares it is not the putting away the filth of
the flefh (the proper work of water) yet they
infift it is water; and fo make it out, if they fub-

C

ftantially

ftantially make out any thing by it, that a figure faves us. Let none therefore marvel that Chrift was fo careful to be baptized in water, in order to fulfil it, before he would go forth publicly into that work, wherein he was to be the baptizer of fouls to falvation; for fince we find that even his fo doing is laid hold of, in direct contradiction to the whole fcope and defign of it, and urged as a proof of its continuance, how much greater would have been the influence of his example, towards continuing a figure in preference to the fubftance, had he firft publifhed his own everlafting gofpel and baptifm, and after that been baptized himfelf in water, and fo baptized others? But as it feems he intended not to baptize others in water, doubtlefs to guard againft the force of example; fo neither would he be fo baptized himfelf, after he had once began his own public and foul-baptizing miniftry; but very carefully did what he had to do in outward fulfilment of that type, both before he began his faid miniftry, and before he had gathered any difciples, yet fo as to be after the reft of the people in thofe parts of the country had been baptized; for it would not have feemed fo proper for him to fubmit to an ordinance that was figurative of his own baptifm, for the fpecial purpofe of fulfilling it, before its adminiftrator had, for fome little time at leaft, practifed it; but now John having baptized many, and raifed their hopes of a more fpiritual and foul-faving baptifm, or, as Luke has it, " when all the people" (meaning doubtlefs there about Jordan) "were baptized, it came to pafs that Jefus alfo being baptized,"

tized," &c. and we do not read of John's ever baptizing another perfon there afterwards.

Now therefore, as already evinced, was the fuitable time for Jefus to be baptized. And though this was done, as before urged, not to perpetuate that fign, but exprefsly to fulfil it, that fo all that kind of ceremonial righteoufnefs might be fulfilled, and not a jot or tittle of it pafs any otherwife away; yet this hindered not the propriety of John's continuing his preaching and fervice in that fign, in other places, a while longer, in order to Chrift's manifeftation, and the preparation of his way before him, there alfo, until nearly the time that Chrift began to publifh the word openly in and from Galilee: though before Chrift would do this, John had, as already proved, finifhed his courfe in that figurative difpenfation, and our Lord had particularly heard of his imprifonment. After which, going into Galilee, he foon entered upon the publication of that fpiritually baptizing word and gofpel miniftration, which, as before obferved, began from thence, after the baptifm which John preached, in the figure.

When John proclaimed, "Behold the Lamb of God," two of John's own difciples immediately "followed Jefus," John i. 36, 37, as did feveral others foon after; for John's preaching, &c. had now in good degree prepared their minds to follow him, as foon as they knew him. But the difciples of John do not appear to have gone from him to Jefus, as from one outward bap-

C 2

tizer

tizer to another. We have no account of
their receiving baptifm in water, after they became followers of Jefus. As that was not his,
but John's, there was no need of repeating it upon
thofe who had. been John's difciples. But had
that of water been Chrift's, and yet diftinct from
John's, they would doubtlefs have received it.
—John's preaching and baptifm in water do
not appear to have prepared the way of the
Lord, by preparing people for a fecond baptifm in water? but by preparing them for that
of the Holy Ghoft, and purifying fire. For
this were fome hearts at leaft, if not many,
now prepared.

Now therefore cometh Jefus to be baptized of
John in Jordan; for it was now time thofe knew
him, who were thus prepared for him, that they
might receive him. His thus coming to John,
and being firft baptized in the type, and then in
the antitype, the Holy Ghoft from heaven, confirmed John's knowledge of him, and gave a
fair occafion for him to point him out, and proclaim him as the baptizer and Saviour of fouls
to the people; thus opening their way to advance from the fign to the fubftance; from the
decreafing miniftration of himfelf, the fervant
and forerunner, to the increafing one of the
Son and Saviour. John could not with full confidence point him out to them, till he knew
him. That could not in proper feafon and fuc-
ceffion take place, by which he certainly knew
him to be the great gofpel Baptizer, till he had
firft baptized him in the figure, feeing the figures
are the fhadows of good things to come after them.

Had

Had Jesus received water baptism much sooner, it had been out of season, and before his way was prepared by his forerunner. Had he deferred it much longer, it had deferred their knowledge and reception of him, whose hearts were now prepared for him.—And, moreover, had he deferred it till John was cast into prison, whence he never came out, he could not have publicly received it by John; by which reception of it from him, and thus rightly timed, he at once confirmed it, as having been a sign of his own; fulfilled it, as of no real use where his own is livingly known; and gave John fair opportunity clearly to know him, and proclaim him the Lamb of God, that taketh away the sins of the world.

Thus John testified of him in due time, agreeably to Paul's expression, 1 Tim. ii. 6, "who gave himself a ransom for all, to be testified in due time." Having seen that Christ's baptism in the figure could be only suffered; seeing the figures precede, point to, but belong not to the gospel, and that now, before the figurative dispensation was abolished, was the only proper and acceptable time for it. Let us observe, who were the only proper persons to fulfil that one peculiar sign and figure of saving baptism—"suffer it to be so now, for thus it becometh us." John, as the ordained administrator of water baptism, and as such, and peculiarly therein, the forerunner of Christ, and Christ, as the end and ender of all types and shadows, were the identical persons to unite in fulfilling this decreasing and terminating dispensation. Hence the divine propriety of the word us: "thus it becometh us." But

what

what to do ? not eftablifh and perpetuate the old
Mofaic inftitutions, in a round of figns and ceremonies, nor any other new or fomewhat varied
obfervations in things outward and fymbolical;
for all thefe are but rudiments, and equally weak
and unappertaining to the pure gofpel ftate.
What then? why, the exact reverfe of all this.
"It becometh us to fulfil;" fulfil what ? "all
righteoufnefs." None of the great and folemn
ordinances of God were fo outward as to be unworthy of fulfilment. All pointed to Chrift, and
to his work and kingdom : but this of water baptifm, as now ufed by John, and by him repeatedly contrafted with Chrift's, or the two placed
by him very pointedly, as type and antitype,
required our Lord's fpecial notice and fulfilment,
previoufly to his own public gofpel miniftration.
And though, as then ufed, it was introduced the
laft in courfe of the great fhadows peculiarly
reprefentative of Chrift's great work in men; yet
was it almoft, if not quite, the firft fpecially
fulfilled by him.

JOHN's miniftration in the fhadow, began too
near the meridian fplendour of Chrift, the gofpel
fun, to have any long continuance previous to
his glorious manifeftation to Ifrael.—Even outwardly, as the fun advances nearer to its meridian
altitude, the length of the fhadow decreafes.
And right under the fun's full blaze, the fun being in its zenith point, fhining on all fides equally, the fhadow vanifhes, or at leaft is under foot.
And I believe it has inwardly, even in refpect of
baptifm, vanifhed quite out of eftimation and
notice in the minds of fome, as the fpiritual fun
has gradually arifen upon them; and who yet
have

have afterwards, through the neglect of a single
eye to the light, gradually receded therefrom, till
(as in the afternoon outwardly) towards night,
in proportion·as the fun's warming and enliven-
ing influence is leffened, the length and unfub-
ftantial importance of the empty fhadow has
greatly increafed with them—they have eagerly
grafped at the fhadow, which in itfelf is nothing
but a likenefs of the fubftance.—We all know a
fhadow outwardly is nothing—and in fpirituals
alfo this is fo ftrictly true, that Paul fays, " circumcifion is nothing, and uncircumcifion is
nothing," 1 Cor. vii. 19; and it holds equally
in outward baptifm, and the fupper.—If one
fhadow were any thing in the gofpel, another
might as well be fomething.—Circumcifion
would be as much fomething as baptifm.—The
gofpel excludes them all.

LET not therefore him who is outwardly baptized fuppofe he has therein fomething that belongs to the gofpel; neither let him who rejects
it, either Quaker or other, think he therefore
has fomething; for outward baptifm is nothing
evangelical, and the mere rejection of it is nothing.—" the new creature," the living faith of
the operation of God, working by love, is all in
all, is the very fubftance of things hoped for,
"the evidence of things not feen," Heb. xi. 1.
Thus neceffary was it for all thefe old things to
pafs away, be fhaken and fulfilled, that the new
and living fubftance, which cannot be fhaken,
may remain.—And as John was the forerunner of
Chrift, and the adminiftrator of water baptifm,
it belonged to him and Jefus; they were the *us*,
to whofe allotment it properly fell to fulfil it.—
Chrift had the typical righteoufnefs of divers

other

other figures to fulfil; hence, afterwards he celebrated the paſſover, and plainly pointed his diſciples to the antitype of it. They muſt eat his
fleſh, and drink his blood, or have no life in them.
And this he aſſures them is ſpiritual, "it is the
ſpirit that quickeneth, the fleſh profiteth nothing," John vi. 63. And even John's work,
in fulfilling theſe things, was not wholly confined
to the outward baptiſm of our Lord. His con-
ſtant teſtimony that his baptiſm was but with
water, as he adminiſtered it to others, his lively
and contradiſtinguiſhing deſcription of Chriſt's, as
that which effects entire ſanctification, and burns
up all the chaff (not only ſin, but figurative ceremonial obſervations; for theſe are as chaff to
the wheat, and as trees that bring not forth any
real good fruits of the goſpel) tended much to
exalt the ſubſtance above all ſigns in the minds of
the people. And when once the ſubſtance is in
due eſtimation, and properly exalted over all in
our minds, under the goſpel, the ſign immediately
loſes its importance, and Chriſt becomes all in
all to us.

But John not only divers times repeats the important diſtinction between baptiſm with water,
and that with the Holy Ghoſt, and holds to view
the comparative inefficacy, and derceaſing nature
and deſign of the one, and the excellency, all-
ſufficiency and increaſing nature of the other: he
degrades all claims of the moſt exact and tenacious adherents to ceremonial inſtitutions, without
the heart-purifying work of the Lord.

Even the zealous phariſees, notwithſtanding
all they could boaſt of relationſhip to Abraham,
either by blood, by circumciſion, or the moſt
ſtrict

ftrict and fcrupulous outward obfervance of the whole law of commandments, contained in (the fhadowy) ordinances, he upbraids as a generation of vipers; and plainly intimates to them, that the true feed of Abraham are they in whom the axe, the fan, and the fire of the gofpel make thorough work; and that in this way God is able to raife up children in the true and living faith of faithful Abraham, of fuch whofe hearts were as ftones. There might be fuch then prefent, whofe difregard to thofe things, wherein lay nearly all the religion of too many of the pharifees, was fuch as to render them extremely obnoxious and contemptible in their view, and who yet were more eafy to be brought in love with the effentials of true religion than they; though they, in the fury of their zeal againft thefe, might ftrikingly exhibit the viper in fpirit. I believe the inward feelings and outward deportment of many, who have confiderable zeal in exteriors, are the very reverfe of this, in meeknefs, gentlenefs and love.

May they experience a bleffed increafe herein; and may all ranks and denominations of Chriftian, beholding the excellency hereof, and its vaft importance, in preference to all party attachments, and zeal for or againft ceremonials, more and more prefs after it and into it themfelves, and cherifh and promote it in each other.

I doubt not many of the pharifees were zeal-oufly obfervant of the Mofaic inftitutions, becaufe they verily believed it was God's will they fhould be fo (as doubtlefs it was in a right way and difpofition.) I doubt not but fome of thefe were moral, goodly fort of men, as to outward regularity, uprightnefs, and honeft dealing, and here
they

they refted, well fatisfied, and defpifed the lefs obfervant, and lefs regular. But here refting (even though they might be, as touching every thing merely ceremonial, or even merely moral, pretty blamelefs) they were and muft be far fhort of that, which in every age of the world has been the true righteoufnefs, riches, and falvation of fouls. Thefe, as well as the more impure and grofsly polluted within, John wanted to alarm, and fhake from their falfe reft, and fig-leaf covering; that they might come to know the pure and living righteoufnefs of faith, that works by love, purifies the heart, gives victory, removes mountains, and is the fubftance, being of the operation of God in the heart; not a mere affent to certain well-eftablifhed facts, nor yet merely a full and firm perfuafion of their truth and certainty; but a real and living hold on Chrift the life, in inward union with him; by a deep and powerful working of the holy principle of light and life in the foul. This is that righte-
· oufnefs which exceeds that of the fcribes and pharifees, and without which Chrift fays we cannot enter into the heavenly kingdom. See Mat. v. 20. This, in fulnefs eftablifhed, fuper-
s cedes all figns and fhadows. Hence John, by rejection of the pharifaical dependence on defcent from Abraham, &c. was preparing his way, who coming after him, had much of this nature to do, among that fuperftitious and bigotted people; who, as he rightly teftified, had they been truly the children of Abraham, would have done the works of Abraham; but not being truly his feed, in the heavenly birth, and holy principle of life and immortality, wherein the joint heirfhip with Chrift ever confifted, they were foolifhly, though zealoufly, endeavouring to climb up fome other
. way;

way; by outward performances, and exact obfervation of ordinances; a kind of righteoufnefs which never gave admittance, or brought into the kingdom. And as men have ever been prone to ftop fhort in thefe, and rely more or lefs upon them, as things of fubftantial benefit in themfelves; God was pleafed, in the fulnefs of . time, to fend his Son, made of a woman, made under the law, and purpofely brought under the obfervance of thefe things, for their fulfilment, in order exprefsly to blot out, remove and take out of the way; that a more fingle attention might take place to the writing of the law in the heart; the very life, fum and fubftance of the new covenant. See Jer. xxxi. 33. John's preaching tended directly to prepare for and introduce an increafing attention to thefe great things within, and thus powerfully contributed to promote that living acquaintance with, and fingle dependence on the fubftance, which is the only thing that ever rightly qualifies the mind to fee beyond, and thoroughly, underftandingly, and profitably renounces and relinquifhes the fign. This was fulfilling his commiffion, preparing the way of the Lord, pointing out, declaring and promoting the decreafe of all figurative righteoufnefs, including even that of his own baptifm; and affifting in the fulfilment thereof, in order to the increafe, eftablifhment and general prevalency of that which was before all figns, and remains to the faithful, the *fummum bonum*, the one good thing needful, the life and fubftance of all true religion.

CHAP.

CHAP. II.

*John's baptifm ftill in ufe after Chrift was baptized;
and on what grounds. Why John muft decreafe.
Why the leaft in the kingdom is greater than he.
Water baptifm never a gofpel ordinance, any more
than burnt offerings, circumcifion, &c. Chrift's
transfiguration clearly fhows all thefe, done
away together, and water baptifm as much as any
of them though afterwards fometimes ufed in
condefcenfion, as divers other figures were. John
feen in the mount as Elias. Peter's conduct
with Cornelius, no perpetuation of water; but
rather a prudent condefcenfion. The full difpenfation of Chrift, is God and man in union.
Man prone to imagery. Signs were ever by
indulgence. A touch upon the paffover. Chrift
eating it, points to its antitype, the inward feaft,
and communion of faints.*

ALTHOUGH on very fufficient grounds, as
already evinced, our bleffed Lord received
that baptifm which was figurative of his own, and
fo far as in that manner behoved him fulfilled it,
previoufly to his entrance on his own public miniftration, in preaching the gofpel, yet for his
further manifeftation to Ifrael in fome other
places,

places, that watery fign, and the preaching accompanying it, were afterwards continued by John, till fome little time before the bleffed Jefus began his faid public miniftry? and the difciples of Jefus having learned that baptifm of John, and understanding it was for their Lord's manifeftation to Ifrael, they alfo practifed it, and doubtlefs with a view and defire of his more extenfive and fpeedy manifeftation among the people; though we have no account that Chrift ever at all encouraged them therein, but an exprefs affurance that he " himfelf baptized not," John iv. 2. Perhaps he might have no objection (as ceremonials were yet in ufe, as a fchool-mafter leading to himfelf, the life and fubftance, the pure gofpel ftate not generally commencing till after his refurrection) to their baptizing others, as John had them, in the figure; well knowing that occafion might thereby be taken to turn the mind profitably from that likenefs of entire cleanfing, to the neceffity of the thing itfelf, his own faving baptifm; and which feems to have been the very defign of water baptifm, as ufed by John. No other need of it feems ever to have exifted; and no other end feems to have been aimed at, by the divine wifdom, in fending John baptizing in that manner. It was to that end well adapted, and to that only.—And that John knew this, feems evident by his declaring that baptifm was for Chrift's manifeftation, by his fo conftantly pointing from it to its antitype,* the baptifm

* The word in the common tranflation rendered figure, 1 Pet. iii. 21; fpeaking of the baptifm which now faves us is antitypon; and furely it is the antitype, and not the type or figure, that is saving.

that

that faves the foul; and by his acknowledgment that himfelf muft decreafe, and Chrift increafe. Had John been the adminiftrator of a gofpel ordinance, and therein abode faithful, he might, inftead of decreafing, have increafed therein: but being the adminiftrator of a figurative ordinance, in its very nature, end and defign, decreafing; he, as its adminiftrator, muft decreafe: for though as great a Prophet as any born of woman, yea, as Chrift declares, " much more than a Prophet," the immediate forerunner and preparer of the way of the Lord; yet truly, as the Lord himfelf further afferts, Mat. xi. 2, " he that is leaft in the kingdom of heaven, is greater than he;" that is, greater than John, as John the Baptift; for it is exprefsly as John the Baptift, that Chrift fays this of him; and in this fenfe it will forever hold true. For though as a faint and fervant of God, as a Prophet of the Moft High, John was great, yea very great in the heavenly kingdom, " a burning and a fhining light," as Chrift ftill further teftifies, John v. 35, yet that gofpel kingdom which John proclaimed as near at hand, and prepared the way for, being void of all mere figurative ordinances, and operating wherever it cometh in its full glory to their fulfilment, abolition, out-blotting, and entire removal out of the way; the leaft in the pure fpirituality thereof, (having feen and advanced, beyond and to the difufe and total rejection of all fuch figns and figures, as being comparatively mean and beggarly elements, of ufe only till the feed came, and at beft but fhadows of the good things to come) is and ever muft be in this refpect greater than John, as John the Baptift; the adminiftrator of one, though a very fignificant one, of thofe figurative ordinances.

ordinances. And even though John fhould' fit
higher, fhine brighter, and be far greater in the
kingdom 'of eternal glory, than many of thefe,
yet as the Baptift, or baptizer in water, he
was under a difpenfation that was vaftly low in
comparifon of that pure gofpel ftate which thefe
little ones all witnefs in the new covenant difpenfation; which water baptifm could no more be
a part of, or belong to, than circumcifion, burnt-
offerings, or any other rituals of the Mofaic difpenfation. And if Mofes, however faithful in
all his houfe, as a fervant, muft as to his law of
ceremonials, his difpenfation of figns and fhadows,
decreafe and give place to the Son, furely fo muft
John. The weaknefs, outwardnefs, and infufficiency, on account of which the fhadows of
Mofes have vanifhed, are as apparent in water
baptifm, as in any of thefe; and it is of as much
real neceffity that this be decreafed, fulfilled, and
ceafe, in order to the true and pure enjoyment of
its antitype, the faving baptifm of Chrift, as that
circumcifion, and the divers wafhings and offerings of the law fhould ceafe, for the fame reafon,
or in order to the right enjoyment of their antitype.

It is rather mournful to fee fo many religious,
good people—people who love God, and are in
good degree enlightened, entangled as it were in
the bondage of outward and typical ordinances,
in thefe antitypical gofpel days. What volumes
of controverfy, and not always in the fweteeft
temper, have been and are written, and from
time to time, even unto this day very zealoufly
fpread, read, and rejoiced in, which yet contain
little or nothing relative to the life of God in the
foul,

foul, the one foul-faving, fanctifying baptifm of
the gofpel, or the one foul-fatiating communion
of faints, and fupper of the Lord; but are filled
with learned or unlearned argumentation, about
things as foreign to the true Chriftian life and
difpenfation, as the facrificing of bullocks, rams,
and lambs !

I feel real tendernefs towards thofe who are
not yet fo tranflated into the glorious liberty of
the fons of God, not yet fo enlightened as to rife
fuperior to their attachments to elementary and
figurative obfervances ; and I wifh not unnecefla-
rily to hurt the feelings of one fincere foul.   I
know fome fuch hold water baptifm, and what
they call the other facrament, in great veneration;
and I do fincerely defire them not to take offence
at my freely endeavouring to evince them to belong not to the gofpel.   It is love in great fin-
cerity that engages me to fhew them that thefe
things ftand exactly on a level with the long ceafed
ceremonials of the law, in point of obligation
under the gofpel.   It would be as ftrictly a gofpel
controverfy, were men now to write volume after
volume refpecting the due and precife manner of
offering the ancient daily facrifice ; as is that
about immerfion and fprinkling, or that refpecting the various opinions and modes of adminiftration in what is called the Lord's fupper. Thou
need have no more, O thou true-hearted Chriftian
traveller, to do with thefe, than the former : it
no more imports to thy real gofpel duty, or thy
growth in the divine life, to underftand and practife in the moft precife manner, according 'to
ancient original inftitution and ufage in thefe, than
in the others. Think of what entire infignificancy

cancy it is, to controvert points refpecting the
offering of the lambs, "one in the morning, the
other at even," as ordained of old to be done
day by day for a continual burnt offering,
Numb. xxviii. 3, 4. Think how unimportant to
difpute, whether a fifth or a tenth part of an
ephah of flour, or whether mingled with a third,
fourth or eighth part of an hin of beaten oil,
would now under the gofpel be the moft acceptable meat offering to the Lord; and thou
mayeft perhaps perceive to obtain a true glimpfe
at leaft of the real infignificancy to thy life
and duty, as a Chriftian, of all the elaborate
enquiries and difcuflions, refpecting either what
is the proper mode, or who are the proper fubjects of either the one or the other of the fa-
craments fo called.

But feeing many pious fouls are yet under the
vail in thefe things, wifhing to ferve God, and
fearing to offend him; and feeing it is much for
the worldly intereft, emolument and popularity
of too many who affume the character and
office of gofpel minifters, to keep them ftill
under this vail and covering, and in bondage
to the beggarly elements; I am willing to ufe my
endeavours to evince yet more fully and clearly
the abfolute ceffation and difmiffion of figns and
fymbols, as never having pertained to the fulnefs of the gofpel ftate. I think this is clearly
exhibited by our Lord at the transfiguration;
and I think it as much includes John as Mofes;
as much water baptifm as circumcifion; and
as much the paffover as burnt offerings. In
fhort, it is evident to my mind, that the whole
tendency and defign of the vifion was to fhew

D   the

the equal difmiffion of all thofe fhadows of the good things to come. And that for this reafon; of all the holy men of old, all the great types of our Immanuel, Mofes and John in the character of Elias appeared, on this wonderful occafion, with Chrift and his difciples in the mount. None elfe would have fully anfwered the defign of the transfiguration. But thefe two, reprefenting the complete body of figns and ceremonies, were the identical perfons to appear and difappear to them, and in teftimony of the difannulling of all thofe foregoing ordinances, as the wafhings, oblations, &c. under Mofes, were but figns, and but until the full coming in of the difpenfation of life and fubftance: and as the baptifm ufed by John was alfo but a fign, fo now, in exhibiting the entire abolition of both, our Lord in fome fort did it by way of fign or reprefentation. And as it requires fome fpiritual difcernment, clearly to perceive that offerings, water baptifm, &c. never were nor could be more than figns and figures, what they were particularly the figns and figures of, how long they were properly ufed, and when utterly abolifhed, fo does it alfo require fome true illumination from on high, to read and underftand the myftery of transfiguration, and to fee plainly that the whole drift and defign of it was, to teach us that the gofpel, the kingdom, the baptifm of Jefus, are all inward and fpiritual, the antitypical righteoufnefs which remains, and ever will remain to the true church; though all that typical righteoufnefs, which Chrift fpake of in his anfwer to John, introductory to his baptifm in the figure, be fulfilled.

WHEN God would fhow Abraham, Gen. xv.
that

that his feed fhould be a ftranger in a land not
theirs, and after four hundred years affliction,
" come out with great fubftance," he ordered
him to take an heifer, fhe goat, ram, turtle
dove, and a young pigeon. Dividing feveral
of thefe in the midft, he " laid each piece one
againft another." And when the fun was going
down a deep fleep fell upon Abraham, and lo,.
" an horror of great darknefs fell upon him ;"
and further it " came to pafs, that when the
fun went down, and it was dark, behold a
fmoaking furnace, and a burning lamp that
paffed between thofe pieces." A very ftriking
reprefentation of Ifrael's iron furnace of affliction
in Egypt, and the burning lamp, or, as the
margin reads, " a lamp of fire," very beautifully
betokened their joyful deliverance, when long
after the angel of the Lord led them by a
" pillar of fire" from the fevere exactions of
their hard-hearted enemies and tafk-mafters.—
Thus dealt infinite wifdom and goodnefs with his
favoured fervant, good old Abraham ; by ftriking reprefentations fhewing him things to come,
and divers other inftances of fomewhat fimilar
reprefentations might be adduced.

But paffing them, we come now to that very
important one, the transfiguration, and to unfold
a little its genuine import and meaning, according
to the degree of underftanding received. I fhall
firft endeavour to evince, that it was John the
Baptift who, with Mofes, appeared in the mount,
though under the denomination and character of
Elias. It is clear that John was the Elias, that
is the Elijah, whom the Lord by the Prophet
promifed to fend to prepare the way of the

Lord,

Lord, Mal. iii. 1, 4, 5. This promife Mark re‑
cites exprefsly as fulfilled in the coming and
fervices of John, Mark i. 2. as it is written in
the Prophets, "behold I fend my meffenger
before thy face, which fhall prepare thy way
before thee.".

THAT this was John, is further evident by
what the angel faid to John's father, good old
Zacharias, Luke i. 16, 17, " many of the children
of Ifrael fhall be turned to the Lord their God—
and he fhall go before him in the fpirit and
power of Elias," &c. Indeed Chrift's own words
are full to the purpofe: he pofitively declares,
Mat. xi. 14, " if ye will receive it, this is
Elias, which was for to come ;" but as he did
not mean that Elias was actually come again
in perfon, but that John was come " in the
power and fpirit of Elias," as before mentioned ;
he adds, verfe 15, knowing how outward the
people's minds were, and how fpiritually dull
they were of hearing, " he that hath ears to
hear, let him hear." He doubtlefs knew that
many could not fo hear as to believe and receive
it, in its naked fignification, efpecially as John
had denied his being Elias. Thefe are contra-
dictions to mere human wifdom : the ear that
underftandingly hears them, the Lord alone
openeth.

JOHN fpake truth from the heart; for when
they afked him, " what then, art thou Elias ?"
John i. 21. they were fo carnal and outward in
their apprehenfions, that doubtlefs John faw they
fo little underftood the fcripture prophefies and
promifes, that they were looking for the perfonal
coming

coming of Elias from heaven; and perhaps in a fiery chariot, his afcenfion, or taking up, having been reprefented as in a chariot of fire. John anfwering their queftion according to their fenfe in afking it, faith, " I am not;" thereby harmonioufly coinciding with Chrift's defign in fpeaking in parables; for Chrift thanked his Father that he had "hid thefe things from the wife and prudent, and revealed them unto babes," Mat. xi. 2, 5. Thefe babes are the fame with thofe who have ears to hear, and Chrift fpake in parables to concur with his Father in hiding thefe things from the pryings and inveftigations of this world's wifdom and prudence: for when "the difciples came and faid unto him, why fpeakeft thou unto them in parables? Mat. xiii. 10. he anfwered and faid unto them," becaufe it is given unto you to know the myfteries of the kingdom of heaven, but to them it is not given," verfe 11. and in conformity to thefe defigns of Chrift and the Father, to make foolifh the wifdom of this world, John anfwered, that he was not Elias; as truly he was not in the fenfe of the queftion, and yet in the fenfe of heaven and of the Holy Ghoft he was indeed Elias, yea, the only Elias that was fent in fulfilment of the promife, to prepare the way of the Lord Jefus. So that had he not come in the power and fpirit of Elias, the promife, for aught that appears, had utterly failed.

THIS point, thus clearly eftablifhed in the facred records, contributes much towards a right underftanding of the transfiguration. The tranf-actions of this ever memorable and important fcene, I have no doubt, were defigned to unfold,

D 3

as

as far as thofe who faw and heard them, or thofe
who fince read them, have "ears to hear," the
deep myftery of the three difpenfations of Mofes,
John, and Jefus—the entire paffing away of all
that was but typical in the two former, as things
liable in their very nature, and in the defigns of
infinite wifdom, ever meant to be fhaken and removed ; that fo the latter, the difpenfation of life
and fubftance, the pure fpiritual unfhadowy gofpel and kingdom of Chrift, as things that cannot
be fhaken or removed, might with greater clearnefs fucceed, and remain.

To this purpofe the Lord of this glorious difpenfation, after teftifying that fome then ftanding
there fhould live to fee it—that is, fhould " not
tafte of death till they had feen the kingdom of
God come with power," Mark ix. 1—in order to
prepare fome of his difciples for a more extenfive
and clear difcovery of its purely fpiritual, antitypical nature and glory, and to give as it were a
clue to the fame difcovery to others (fee Mat. xvii.
Mark ix. Luke ix.) in that and after ages, "taketh
with him Peter, and James, and John" (three
eminent inftruments in the primitive church)
" and leadeth them up into an high mountain,
apart by themfelves." This may fhew us, that
in order to a clear reception of divine knowledge,
our minds muft both afcend above and be feparated from the bufy fcenes of mere earthly joys,
cares, and affociations, as it were into the
mount of fequeftration, into an holy abftrac-
tion of foul, where angels afcend and defcend,
and the converfe is at times with God. " He
that hath ears to hear, let him hear." Here
our Lord " was transfigured before them, and his
raiment

raiment became fhining, exceeding white as fnow, fo as no fuller on earth can white them. And there appeared unto them Elias, with Mofes, and they were talking with Jefus. And Peter anfwered and faid to " Jefus, Mafter, it is good for us to be here." Alas! too many think it is good to retain the long fince fulfilled and abrogated fymbols of good things, to this very day; and not content with, or not enough acquainted with the one true " tabernacle of God, that is inwardly with men," Rev. xxi. 3. are, with Peter, for building three, in order to retain a little from the ceremonies of Mofes, as the paff-over (which they dignify with the name of the Lord's fupper) and a little from John (here feen as Elias, in whofe life, power, and fpirit, John came) to wit, water baptifm. So Peter, igno-rantly thinking it good to remain where all three might have place together, propofeth, or afks liberty, as followeth: " let us make three taber-nacles, one for thee, one for Mofes, and one for Elias; for he wift not what to fay," Mark ix. 2. 7. In very deed, he wift not, or, according to Luke's account, knew not what he faid: knew not that this propofal ftruck directly againft the fimplicity of the gofpel, and was contrary to the life and defign of the transfiguration.

He was for buildings which belong not to the gofpel day; tabernacles for thofe whofe difpen-fations were but preparatory to that which is purely of Jefus: for there was a cloud that over-fhadowed them. Oh! that it may be feen, and daily confidered, how exactly this is the cafe now, with thofe who ftill think it good to re-main under the fhadows. Is not the cloud ftill over them? The figns under Mofes and John

(here

(here Elias) pointed men to Chrift; but the full difpenfation of Jefus, is nothing fhort of God and man in heavenly union. As then in him, fo now, in all the feed, all his true difciples, there is a real joining and uniting of the life of man in and with the life of God in the foul. "He that is joined to the Lord is one fpirit," Cor. vi. 17.

THIS is livingly taught us in the Chrift of God, being truly both the Son of God and the Son of Man. Here all preceding difpenfations end; the figns are fuperceded; Chrift becomes our one life in the heavenly fellowfhip, and, as Paul fays, "I live; yet not I, but Chrift liveth in me," Gal. ii. 20. Here we enjoy the true riches and glory of his inheritance in the faints, which is Chrift in us the hope of glory. See Eph. i. 18. Col. i. 27.—What can all the fhadows of the good things to come do for thofe who poffefs and enjoy the good things themfelves, are led unto, live and act in the life and fubftance pointed at by all the types and figures of old? Did Chriftians know and enjoy this myftery in its true fulnefs and glory, all old things would be done away; for here all things become new; all things of God; here we are complete in Jefus, in whom the fulnefs dwells; and have no need at all of figns to perfect us in our Chriftian duty: no need of outward wafhing, being wafhed in his blood, inwardly fprinkled, to the cleanfing of the heart: no need of outward circumcifion—our circumcifion and baptifm are in Chrift —into death with him, putting off the body of the fins of the flefh: no need of eating bread and drinking wine, in remembrance of him, feeing he has become our life; we enjoy his foul-fatiating

ing, his all' confolating prefence—he fups with
us, and we with him—eating the bread of
life, and drinking the new wine of falvation
with us in the heavenly kingdom of his Father,
inwardly and fpiritually—where all types ceafe
for ever---where the faith which is the very fubftance of things hoped for, the new creature in
this union of God and man, is all in all.—Here
every thought is " brought into captivity to the
obedience of Chrift," 2 Cor. x. 5. No mere outward obfervations can add any thing ufeful to
this ftate; and this is the reafon why they muft and
do here ceafe. The reafon why they were once
ufed was, that men were too much alienated from
the life and fubftance—they were ufed as outward
pointers to the inward life.—When the refurrection of Chrift, the life is fully known in us, all
mere figns are, and in the very nature of things,
muft be, entirely fuperceded. Till then, we
may be in a ftate of mixture, as many are with
their three tabernacles, one for Jefus, one for
John, and one for Mofes. Hence the figurative
difpenfation was not altogether abolifhed outwardly, till Chrift's outward refurrection; this
being generally the cafe in the inward. Thofe
who have not known this pretty fully in themfelves, are moftly fome way or other relying more
or lefs on outward things; but they whofe life
is fully and truly in him, who is the refurrection
and the life, are got beyond all improper reliance
on any thing but the life of Jefus in them—this is
the plain reafon why the antitypical baptifm,
which now faves us, is by the refurrection of
Chrift---not by wafhing in water to put away the
filth of the flefh---for though fome of the tranf-
lators ufe the word figure in a text which fpeaks
                                          plainly

plainly of this fpiritual baptifm, it is not fo in the
Greek. The original word, as already noted, is
antitypon: fo that the faving baptifm, there
fpoken of, and which is by the refurrection and
life of Chrift, is not a figure, but the very antitype itfelf.---Had Peter known this at the time
of the transfiguration, as well as he did when he
wrote his epiftles, it is in no wife probable that
he would have thought the building of tabernacles, for the retention of figns and fhadows, a
gofpel labour: but feeing Peter was as yet fo far
from a clear underftanding of the nature and pure
fpirituality of the gofpel, as to propofe three
tabernacles even then, juft when Chrift was fpecially opening the difmiffion of all but one, that
is " the tabernacle of God, that " is with men,"
Rev. xxi. 3; let none marvel that this fame Peter
afterwards commanded the houfhold of Cornelius
to be baptized in water, a thing in no wife
ftrange for him to do, even though it had not
been done merely in condefcenfion, as there is
much reafon to believe it was. He remained
for fome time too outward and limited in his
ideas; he did not know that the gofpel was an
univerfal thing, extending to Gentiles as well as
Jews---fo that a wonderful vifion was vouchfafed,
to remove his fcruples, and induce his vifit to
Cornelius—and when there, God gave him words
fuitable to the occafion, and which being delivered in the evidence and demonftration of the
Spirit, and with divine power, were eminently
inftrumental to their baptifm with the Holy
Ghoft who heard him, even in fuch a remakable
manner, that at his firft utterance, as he began
to fpeak, the Holy Ghoft fell on them.

THIS

THIS at once ftruck Peter, as being an exact and gracious performance of the promiffory word of the Lord Jefus—" John indeed baptized with water, but ye fhall be baptized with the Holy Ghoft." See Acts xi. 15, 16. For this baptifm was now fo evidently difpenfed through Peter's preaching, that he immediately remembered this precious promife of our bleffed Lord—which had been very illy applied by him to the Holy Ghoft falling on them, had that not been ftrictly the baptifm of the Holy Ghoft, as intended by the promife—nor indeed can any, who clearly know this baptifm, think ftrange of Peter's recollecting this promife, and applying it to what took place at this memorable feafon; nor is there any doubt with me but that the Holy Ghoft brought it to his remembrance, and fhewed him it was now actually performed through himfelf as an inftrument; for God had truly and eminently enabled him to execute, in a very exact and ftriking manner, the great commiffion of our Lord, Mat. xxviii. 19. which was to teach, baptizing; not teach, and then baptize, as two feparate acts; but by teaching in the power and efficacy received from on high, they were to baptize them into the very name, that is the life and power, of the Father, Son, and Holy Ghoft.—And into this name, life and power, Peter did baptize them: they received it as he fpake unto them, which exactly anfwered the commiffion, " teach, baptizing."

No marvel, then, that he immediately remembered Chrift's promife, " ye fhall be baptized with the Holy Ghoft"—feeing the baptifmal influences thereof, attendant upon his power-

ful

ful preaching, were fo livingly in fulfilment
thereof.—Neverthelefs, as water had been in
great eftimation, it feems Peter thought beft to
condefcend to the weaknefs of thofe young converts, and of his Jewifh brethern then prefent,
as his Lord and Mafter had again and again
gracioufly condefcended to him in his weaknefs.
—So he commanded them to be baptized; and
perhaps he could not have done better in their
weak ftate, and efpecially. as none appeared to
forbid it, which it is probable he might not
know but fome then prefent might have authority
to do; for his mind began now to be confider-
ably enlarged; he clearly perceived (which he
feems not to have known before) that God was
no refpecter of perfons, of Jew more than Gentile, &c. Indeed the very query, " can any man
forbid water ?" &c. Acts x. 47. is an appeal to
men, and befpeaks a ftate of hefitation, or
uncertainty. Nor is his hefitancy at all to,
be admired at, things having fo wonderfully
altered in his view in a fhort time paft; and the
anointing of truth, that brings all things to
remembrance, having juft now revived in his
mind the fweet and precious promife of his dear
Redeemer—"John indeed baptized with water,
but ye fhall be baptized with the Holy Ghoft,"
which he could not but fee and know, was then,
through him, gracioufly taking place upon thefe
Gentiles; it is by no means ftrange that he
doubted the propriety of baptizing them in water.
It had been much ftranger, had he not doubted
it, efpecially. as water was the very thing which
our Lord, in the words now brought to Peter's
remembrance, had pointedly oppofed to his own
baptifm; that, as a thing which had been; his

own,

own, as what fhould be : Peter therefore plainly
feeing the latter, might well doubt the further
ufe of the former, efpecially among Gentiles,
feeing its very defign was that Chrift might be
manifeft to Ifrael.

CORNELIUS and his family were not of Ifrael;
and if they had been, why continue the fign in
prefence of the fubftance, unlefs in condefcenfion
to the weaknefs that could not readily relinquifh
it ? It is evident enough that Peter did not think
it indifpenfible, or he would fcarcely have put
the queftion at all.—There is very little room in
propriety to afk another whether that can be for-
bidden, which we know ourfelves we are indif-
penfibly enjoined and commanded.—Water baptifm was not at that time in force; yet Peter
might rationally doubt whether it would give
fatisfaction to omit it, and fo might cautioufly
put the queftion, to feel out their minds; not
really knowing but that fome one prefent might
fo livingly open its abolition, and fo fatisfyingly
declare its non-effentiality, that all the reft would
have been perfectly fatisfied with the omiffion of
it.—But none doing this, and it being a new cafe,
Peter it feems, defirous of getting through fafely,
and without hurting any tender mind, and knowing that his now commanding it done need not
perpetuate it (nor does it, any more than James,
directing to anoint the fick with oil in the name
of the Lord, perpetuates that) but that after
mature confideration, and when the ftate of
things would bear it, it might be quite laid afide,
did on this occafion command it to be done; and
it might really be fafeft and beft, at that time, fo
to do; nor was this and the anointing with oil
the

the only ceremonies that were still at times condefcendingly ufed, fome time after the abrogation of figns and figures, as to any further obligation.

A well-timed condefcenfion to the weaknefs of others, is an excellent thing—but let none now delight to dwell in the weaknefs, and therein weakly confider the condefcenfion exercifed at a time, wherein it was evidently a very nice and difficult point to know how to proceed fo as to hurt no one, either Jew or Greek; as eftablifhing an ordinance of perpetual obligation under the gofpel, that difpenfation of life and fubftance pointed to, by fuch outward obfervation. For fo far is that condefcenfion from affording any juft pretence for fuch a conclufion, that we have great reafon to believe that even Peter himfelf, foon after this, became quite clear to omit water baptifm entirely, as a figurative thing, not belonging to the gofpel; for we do not find he ever afterwards once ufed or ordered it to be adminiftered to any; but on the contrary, we do find he defcribes the baptifm that now faves us as quite another thing, and as being effected by the refurrection of Chrift the life, to the anfwer of a good confcience. And indeed it muft be fo; for the gofpel of Chrift is, and in its own pure nature muft be, void of any mere outward and figurative obfervations— and to hold it forth fo, in its genuine purity, and ftripped of all thefe figns of both John and Mofes: —we find there was a voice heard out of the cloud, juft after Peter's propofal to build three tabernacles, at the time of the transfiguration, Mat. xvii. Mark ix. Luke ix. 28, &c. faying, "this is my beloved Son, hear him," 35. A very

timely

timely admonition indeed, and sufficient, one might suppose, to prevent all who understand it from wishing to build three tabernacles, or to retain any of the mere shadows of either Moses or John, as circumcision, the passover, or water baptism, now, since they are all ended, and Christ is to be heard in all things.

WHILST the cloud overshadowed them, they were for three tabernacles (they knew not that Moses and John must not be retained) but when the divine voice brake through the cloud, they had their attention called singly to Jesus. But further, that no confirmation should be wanting, and as it were in order to set it home, and seal it for ever, that this was the true intent and meaning of this glorious vision, and of the voice from the excellent glory, we find that immediately upon their hearing said voice, even " suddenly when they had looked round about, they saw no man any more, save Jesus only, with themselves."

HERE is the genuine simplicity of Christ's spiritual kingdom and gospel beautifully and instructively displayed.—Here those things that were of a nature, and in design, to be shaken, fulfilled and done away, are removed; and that only which cannot be shaken remains. This is shaking not the earth only, but also heaven; not sin, and carnality, and earthly-mindedness alone; but here a great part of many people's religion, and what they think belongs to the very kingdom of heaven, and gospel of Jesus, are shaken and removed out of the way; yea, things once of God himself ordained, as striking shadows of the good things to come, but ever by him designed

to

to vanifh, in the full prefence and enjoyment of
the good things themfelves. Bleffed are they
who " have ears to hear," and hearts to underftand, and faith to follow the Lamb of God where-
foever he leadeth, even to the lofs of all their
own buildings, their own righteoufnefs, and
creaturely perfomances, till they come to ceafe
from their own works, as God did from his.—
Thefe fhall be eftablifhed as Mount Sion, that
fhall never be removed; and being preferved
from fubjecton to, or from touching, tafting or
handling, thofe outward ordinances, which confift in things that perifh with the ufing, fhall
know the Lord to be one, and his name one;
and living and ferving the one Lord, in the life,
love and victory of the faints' one true faith,
fhall know affuredly that there is but one true
gofpel baptifm, " not the putting away the filth
of the flefh (or outward body, which is the work
of outward wafhing) but the anfwer of a good
confcience towards God, by the refurrection
of Jefus Chrift."—For thefe fhall know him to
be " the refurrection and the life" to and in their
own fouls: Chrift in them the hope of glory,
and fhall have no hope or confidence in any outward fprinklings or dippings, eatings or drinkings, as pertaining to the work of falvation.

The fubftantial " anfwer of a good confcience"
is not known without the refurrection of Chrift in
the foul; but this known in fulnefs ever makes
" perfect, as pertaining to the confcience;"
which yet cannot be experienced but through the
putting off the body of the fins of the flefh.
" For though the baptifm that faves, is not the
putting

putting away the filth of the flesh," that is, the outward filth of the body; yet it ever does put away the finful filth of the fleshly mind; this is the very work and defign of it. Hence its adminiftrator has his fan in his hand, to winnow the chaff from the wheat; his foap, like the fuller, to wash and cleanfe away the filth; and his fire, like the refiner, to feparate the drofs from the gold; yea, purely to purge away all the drofs, tin and even reprobate filver, and burn up the chaff with unquenchable fire; thus cleanfing, and that thoroughly, the very floor of the heart.—This is the baptifm that faves, the work of him who faves " his people from their fins," not in them. It is therefore altogether befide the true meaning of Peter's words, " not the putting away the filth of the flesh," to fuppofe he meant that the faving baptifm he there fpake of does not cleanfe from fin, or put away our finful filth; but that it is an outward ordinance, which muft be fubmitted to, juft to anfwer a good confcience in that particular refpect, without any reliance upon it as to fanctification from fin; which conftruction I have often known it gloffed with, by the pleaders for elementary baptifm.

But is it not ftrange, that men of fenfe fhould confent to believe, that the baptifm which now faveth us, doth not fave us from fin, doth not put away the finful filth of the flesh? If Peter fpake truth when he faid " baptifm doth alfo now fave us," he muft fpeak of the one faving baptifm. There never was but one thing that could fave: " according to his mercy he faved us, by the wafhing of regeneration, and renewing of the Holy Ghoft." Where this is livingly witneffed, " the refurrection and the life" of Chrift is

E   always

always known, and therein "the anfwer of a good confcience towards God" takes place, to a degree of unfpeakable enjoyment; a fulnefs of divine confolation, unknown in the performance of mere outward ordinances, and never attained to but by being planted in the likenefs of Chrift's death, buried with him by true Chriftian baptifm into the death of fin, and this death, by the power of the eternal Spirit, arifing with him in the power of his refurrection, and walking with him in newnefs of life.

But to return; as thofe outward things which had been "impofed until the time of reformation," and were here exhibited, in the transfiguration, as not belonging to the gofpel, were not abfolutely and entirely out of date till Chrift had rifen: he fo far condefcended to their continuance, that he did not forbid and prevent his difciples baptizing his followers in water; for this was a performance at that time in very great vogue, and Chrift well knew how to deal with a people habituated to outward obfervances. It had all along, under the law and prophets, been found extremely difficult to reftrain that people from the idolatries of the heathen, even though God had fo far accommodated himfelf or his law to their outward ftate and difpofition, as to provide them with many figns and ceremonies, "divers wafhings," a worldly fanctuary, &c. Heb. ix. 1.

The mind of man once turned to religious exercifes, and preffing on therein, is hard to be properly reftrained, is very prone to imagery, idolatry, and a great deal of outward fhow and activity. And from this ground fprang all pagan idolatry,

idolatry; all advances toward it among the Jews; all continuations of jewifh, heathenifh or other mere outward figns and fhadows among Chriftians, and many abfurd and foolifh obfervations among Turks and Mahometans. Chrift knew what was in man, and needed none "to teftify" unto him "of man," as appears by John ii. 25. And as he had many things to fay unto his difciples, which they could not at firft bear (fee John xvi. 12) he advanced them gradually, condefcending to their weaknefs, and attachment to things that belong not to, and can have no place in the pure fpirituality of his kingdom. This amply accounts for his difciples continuing to baptize many new difciples, as they came to believe on him, and follow him, even after he and John had in great degree fulfilled that difpenfation; a difpenfation which probably had never been neceffary, but for the dark and untoward ftate of the people's minds. And had they all, when Chrift came, turned their attention rightly to him, and fully underftood the inward and fpiritual nature of his gofpel, there would have been very little if any real ufe for baptifm in water afterwards.

A difpenfation of figns was ever in condefcenfion to man's weaknefs; and once indulged, they are apt to obtain too great veneration, and be too long retained; for it is feldom if ever the cafe, that things highly efteemed, can be dropt all at once fuddenly.—It is often fafer, and better, to lead people along gradually from figns to fubftance, as they can bear it. Therefore the early followers of the bleffed Jefus were tenderly indulged, and all outward things were not at once rent

from

from them; for though he plainly taught (Luke xvii. 20) that the "kingdom of God cometh not with obfervation," or as in the margin, "with outward fhow," yet during the twilight of things, or the evening time, wherein, though there was some light, yet there was alfo fome darknefs; things not being yet wholly clear, nor wholly dark; not yet full and perfect gofpel day, nor altogether night. See Zechar. xiv. 6. 7. He might fafely, and he did wifely permit things not properly belonging to his kingdom, but which were to decreafe, and terminate as the fun arofe, and the day advanced in its full clearnefs and perfection. And thefe things, though then only permitted in condefcenfion, too many very fincere, but in this refpect weak Chriftians, have been gleaning up, from that day to this, inftead of prefling into the fpiritual holy of holies, beyond all vails, figns and fymbols.

They puzzle themfelves with the Apoftles condefcending practices, and would erect thefe into gofpel ordinances, though neither Chrift nor any of his Apoftles ever enjoined their obfervance as fuch. Indeed they were fo far beneath the fpirituality and pure fimplicity of the new covenant, which was and is in the heart and inward parts, that the great Mediator thereof never condefcended, that we have any account of, to baptize one perfon with water; it is on the contrary exprefsly declared, that "Jefus himfelf baptized not, but his difciples." Oh! he well knew why he omitted it; for had he done it, it might have induced his moft enlightened followers to continue it, out of veneration to his example; as many now do from that of his difciples, though

he

he himfelf never once practifed nor commanded it; and though Paul thanked God he had baptized fo very few. See 1 Cor. i. 14.

As to its permiffion during the time after it was in a good degree fulfilled, till Chrift arofe from the dead, it might very well be fuffered in condefcenfion; for the gofpel day and difpenfation had not then fully come in: all that fpace was a time of unfulfilling: many things of an outward typical nature were during that time fulfilled, and very efpecially that of the paffover, which Chrift defired with great defire to eat with his difciples before he fuffered. See Luke xxii. 15. But why was he fo earneft to do it before he fuffered ?—The reafon of this his earneft defire is plain to him " who has ears to hear," to others it may be a myftery. Chrift could never do it with propriety, unlefs before he fuffered; and had he not done it, it would have remained unfulfilled, as to his actual fulfilment, by that fpecial participation of it. It belonged only to the law; it vanifhed with Mofes, as water baptifm did with Elias, that is John; hence it behoved Chrift, in order to its fulfilment; to eat it before he fuffered; while things were fulfilling; whilft the outward and typical things concerning him were having their end (fee verfe 37 of this fame chapter) that fo having done away all thefe things, he might triumph over them, nailing them to his crofs (fee Col. ii. 14.) and be able on the crofs to fay as he did, " it is finifhed," John xix. 30; which he could not have faid with equal propriety, had fo important a type as the paffover remained unabolifhed by him ; and yet many are ignorantly celebrating the paffover very frequent-

ly,

ly, under an idea that Chrift, at the very time
when he ended it, inftituted an outward fupper
of perpetual continuance in his church, which
could not poffibly be, confiftently with the nature
of his kingdom, which is an inward thing; and
therefore, when he fent his difciples to prepare for
him to eat the paffover, he bid them fay, " my
time is at hand, I will keep the paffover at thy
houfe with my difciples," Mat. xxvi. 18. He
knew the time was at hand for all thefe things to
be abolifhed, and have an end, Luke xxii. 37.
He fteadily calls it the paffover, and never, I
think, once by any other name; and having
eaten it with his difciples, and turned their attention to its myftical fignification, to the neceffity
of their eating his fpiritual flefh, and drinking his
fpiritual blood, which, that he might take occafion to do, that they might live by him, was
doubtlefs one great caufe of his anxious defire to
eat it with them, and juft reminded them, in
eating the mere figure, to do it in remembrance
of him; he then, as if purpofely to fhew them it
belonged not to the gofpel, wound up the ceremony, telling them he would not any more eat
or drink thefe outward fymbols, nor partake
again with them of the paffover, till he drank
the wine new with them in the kingdom of
heaven (fee Mat. xxvi. 29.) or until it be fulfilled
in the kingdom of God, Luke xxii. 16; or, as
expreffed verfe 18, " until the kingdom of God
fhall come." This new wine he drank with
them eminently in that holy and fpiritual kingdom, which they lived to fee come before they
tafted of death, according to his promife, on
the day of Pentecoft and other bleffed feafons—
continues to drink it new in the fame glorious
kingdom

kingdom with all that open and let him come in,
for he fups with them, and they with him; and
this is the only true celebration of the Lord's
fupper—that which is outward is not (and cannot
be) to eat the Lord's fupper; for that is fpiritual;
no fuch fign and fymbols can now have any
proper place in Chrift's kingdom—but as he is
fubftantially and experimentally in and with his
people to the end of the world, Mat. xxviii.
20; as he does not leave them comfortlefs, but
cometh unto them, John xiv. 18; as he and
his Father make their real and living abode with
them (fee verfe 23.) fo he eats and drinks with
them in his invifible kingdom, where they " fit
together in heavenly places in Chrift Jefus,"
which can be only in that kingdom. There they
fit under their own vine and fig-tree, where none
can make them afraid; See Mic. iv. 4. Thefe
eat the flefh and drink the blood of the Son of
God, whereby their fouls are made alive.

"WHAT is the chaff to the wheat? faith the
Lord," Jer. xxiii. 28. What is a little bit of
outward bread, and a cup of wine, at beft taken
by way of remembrance, to the real fupper of
the Lord, which all the faints partake of, and
live by? and what if Chrift did tell his difciples,
as they then ate the outward fign, to do it in remembrance of him, Luke xxii. 19; and what
if Paul told them, as often as they did fo, they
fhewed the Lord's death till he came," 1 Cor. xi.
26: furely that makes no inftitution of a perpetual outward ordinance in the church of Chrift.
It was a matter of liberty and choice, whether
after that once they ate it or not; and that but
until the Lord came, according to his promife

E 4   that

that he would not leave them comfortlefs, but would come unto them. And furely they greatly mifs the true end and defign of it, who are ftill in thefe days eating and drinking the outward figure, not difcerning the Lord's fpiritual body, nor partaking of that divine flefh and blood that gives life, nourifhment and vigour to the foul: for if this was their happy experience and enjoyment, in the prefence, company and kingdom of the Lord, with true, living and fenfible difcernment of his body, and that fpiritually broken for them, and of his fpiritual blood, livingly and life-givingly fhed for them; why fhould they be ftill eating and drinking the old, long-ceafed fymbols of it, in remembrance of a prefent Lord and Saviour? Does not this practice befpeak Chrift's real abfence to their fouls, or their non-difcernment of his fpiritual body? Let the wife in heart among them ponder it well.

But now to return to water baptifm: I was mentioning that it might be continued till Chrift's refurrection, with fome kind of indulgent propriety—and accordingly we find, that as they came down from the mountain (after the transfiguration) he (Chrift) charged them that they fhould tell no man what things they had feen, till the Son of Man were rifen from the dead," Mark ix. 9. The vifion looked forward to that time, for the full completion of the things it was defigned to exhibit—and therefore this very filence enjoined on them till that time, is a further and loud confirmation that the foregoing is the genuine import and meaning of the whole vifion; but further they afked him, faying, " why

"why fay the Scribes that Elias muft firft come?"
verfe 11.   And he anfwered and told them,
"Elias verily firft cometh, and reftoreth all things,"
verfe 12: "but I fay unto you, that Elias is indeed come," verfe 13, or, as Matthew has it,
chap. xvii. ver. 12, 13. "but I fay unto you, that
Elias has come already, and they knew him not,
but have done unto him whatfoever they lifted:
likewife fhall alfo the Son of Man fuffer of them"
—then the difciples underftood that he fpake unto
them of John the Baptift; thus clear it is that
John the Baptift was Elias, who had thus appeared
and difappeared in the mount with them: on the
whole, it is evident to thoroughly enlightened
minds as any doctrine in the gofpel, that neither
water baptifm, eating material bread and wine,
nor any other mere outward performance, can
poffibly in the nature of things have any place as
ftanding ordinances in the church and kingdom
of Chrift.   Chrift's coming was defigned to put
an end to all thefe things—and therefore the
eating, drinking, wafhing and purification, which
remain in the gofpel ftate, are all inward and
fpiritual, and can be no otherwife.   The one gofpel baptifm is not that which puts away the outward filth of the flefh (which is all that water can
do (but it is that which actually faves us, and
brings to "the anfwer of a good confcience towards God by the refurrection of Jefus Chrift," 1
Pet. iii. 21.—This no figure could or ever can do
though fuch as continue under the figns of former
difpenfations would have us believe, that the
Apoftle here affirms that a figure faves us, by
the refurrection of Chrift; whereas there never
was and never can be but one thing that faves
the foul, and that is the inward purifying baptifm

tifm of the Holy Ghoft, as Titus iii. 5, "according to his mercy he faved us, by the wafhing of regeneration, and renewing of the Holy Ghoft." Here is fomething that changes, regenerates and renews the foul; well may this be faid to be faving: and as this "wafhing of water by the word" fpiritually faves the foul, how natural is Peter's comparifon of an outward falvation, in an outward ark, on the outward water, to this inward falvation, by inward and fpiritual water, in the inward and fpiritual ark of the everlafting covenant. See Rev. xi. 19. "And the temple of God was opened in heaven, and there was feen in his temple the ark of his teftament," &c. If Chriftians would wait to fee the temple of God thus fpiritually opened in heaven, they would come to know this ark, and would rejoice in the falvation therein experienced; and would know it to be as impoffible for one fign or figure to fave the foul as another; that outward water can no more be fanctified to the wafhing away fin, than the "blood of bulls and of goats," which the Apoftle fays plainly is impoffible, Heb. x. 4, "for it is not poffible that the blood of bulls and of goats fhould take away fins," and it will forever remain as impoffible for outward wafhing to do it—and therefore Peter wifely adds, after mentioning the baptifm that now faves us, "not the putting away the filth of the flefh;" for he had now learned, whatever he had when he vifited Cornelius, and it is likely he pretty well knew it then, that outward water could not wafh away fin, nor "make the comers thereunto perfect, as pertaining to the confcience," any more than the other figns and divers wafhings under

the

the law; and therefore having mentioned outward water in the preceding verſe, left any ſhould
ignorantly ſuppoſe he meant outward water, in
ſpeaking of the baptiſm which now ſaves us, he
carefully and immediately diſtinguiſhes, and declares he did not mean any outward cleanſing,
but ſomething which really doth ſave; and he
aſſerts it to be " by the reſurrection of Jeſus
Chriſt," as that which livingly known in us,
" the reſurrection and the life," brings to the
comfortable anſwer of a good conſcience; and
nothing elſe ever can, for " the law made nothing
perfect" as pertaining to the conſcience; for,
it having a ſhadow of good things to come,
and not the very image of the things, can never,
with thoſe ſacrifices which they offered year by
year continually, make the comers thereunto perfect; for then would they not have ceaſed to be
offered, becauſe that the worſhippers once purg-
ed, ſhould have had no more conſcience of ſins,
Heb. x. 1, 2.

Here we ſee thoſe outward ſacrifices and waſhings, " the ſhadows of good things to come,"
could never purge the conſcience then; nor can
any outward baptiſms, nor all the waters of
Jordan, any more do it now; and therefore Peter,
ſpeaking of the baptiſm which now ſaves us,
brings it home to that which alone can truly purge
the conſcience, and " make the comers thereunto
perfect;" to wit, the bringing in of a better hope,
by the which we draw nigh unto God, Heb. vii.
19. Here we " lay hold upon the hope ſet before
us; which hope" (ſays the Apoſtle) " we have
as an anchor of the ſoul, both ſure and ſteadfaſt,
and which entereth into that within the vail,"

chap.

chap. vi. 18, 19. This is "Chrift in us the hope of glory." See Col. i. 27. This is known only where Chrift is "the refurrection and the life" experimentally to the foul, as before obferved. Here alone is the anfwer of a good confcience; hereby indeed "we draw nigh unto God," and this is all within, and is the experience of fuch only whofe underftandings are fo enlightened, as to "know what is the hope of this calling, and what the riches of the glory of his inheritance in the faints," Eph. i. 18.

CHAP.

C H A P. III.

All old things done away in the gospel state. Signs and shadows ceased. Their use was from men's alienation from Christ; the law being added because of transgression. Christ in men, the life of all dispensations. All change in these, but in accommodation to the change in men. Shadows but imposed until the time of reformation. The way into the holiest of all not manifest, whilst the first tabernacle was standing, and the mind resting in outward ordinances. Water baptism was under the first covenant, and no part *of the second. Hence the least, purely under the second, is greater than John, as John the Baptist. As Moses gave place to Joshua, so John to Jesus. Moses entered not into Canaan; nor John, as the* Baptist, *into the purely spiritual kingdom. Signs and figures make none perfect. Hence there is a disannulling of all these for their* weakness. *It is idle to suppose one set of ceremonials abolished, to make way for others as gospel ordinances. Christ commissionates his disciples, at Galilee, to baptize into the very name, the* life and power *of* God; *not as a separate act, but by their powerful gospel ministry.* They were to teach baptizingly.

AS I have long seen, with sorrow, how the shadows detain people from the substance, and how hard many strive, even against lively convictions

convictions to the contrary, at times, and greatly to their own lofs, in regard to the true riches, glory and inheritance of and in the faints, to make thefe outward things anfwer, as a fubftitute, inftead of inward fubftance; I am in earneft to affift them, if poffible, in the neceffary difcovery that thefe things have long ago ceafed, as to their proper ufe; and can have no proper place in the full funfhine of the gofpel day. Bear with me; therefore, friendly reader, whilft I further fhow how "all old things" (figns and ceremonies) "are paffed away" to all thorough Chriftians, "all things are" (to thefe) "become new; all things are of God," 2 Cor. xvii. 18.

Now it is clear to me, "all old things" are not paffed away, in the experience of any who are continuing in the religious ufe of outward bread, wine, water, or any of the old figurative things of the former difpenfations. The law was added becaufe of tranfgreffions, till the feed fhould come, Gal. iii. xix. If man had not tranfgreffed againft the light of Chrift, fhining in the heart, and enlightening "every man that cometh into the world" (John i.) I fuppofe no outward written law had ever been neceffary. Were not the minds of men alienated from the life and government of Chrift in the foul, where the kingdom of heaven is (for Chrift declares it is within) none of the figns, either of John's or the Mofaic difpenfation, had ever been found needful. Thefe were only as a fchoolmafter, to lead the mind back from its wanderings "to Chrift, who is the fame yefterday, to day, and forever;" the change is only in us, and all the change of difpenfations, from firft to laft, is in accommodation and condefcenfion to the chang-
ing

ing and changed ftate of men. Chrift was " before Abraham," and was and is all the real life, in and under every difpenfation; and thofe outward things were only "impofed on them until the time of reformation" (Heb. ix. 10) until a return to that from which the mind was enftranged, for in that enftranged, bewildered and outward literal ftate of mind, the way into the holieft of all was not made manifeft;" for the firft, the outward " tabernacle, was yet ftanding," verfe 8; and the mind in this ftate was ftill difpofed to ftop and reft in the outward tabernacle, and in the fhadow of the firft covenant, "which had many ordinances of divine fervice, and a worldly fanctuary." See verfe 1. Here the outward worfhippers refted fecure, although this tabernacle was but " a figure for the time then prefent, in which were offered both gifts and facrifices, that could not make him that did the fervice perfect, as per-taining to the confcience, which ftood only (let it be duly noticed) in meats, and drinks, and divers wafhings and carnal ordinances impofed on them, until the time of reformation," verfe 10. But none of thefe things belong to the gofpel, or times of real reformation, and full return to the life and fubftance, which was of old, before ever the outward law was written, amply fufficient for all that would keep to it. But men departing from this, and rebelling againft the light, they know not the ways thereof, nor abide in the paths thereof, Job xxiv. 13 And in this alienated and rebellious ftate " the law entered, that the offence might abound," Rom. v. 20; for God, in gracious condefcenfion to man thus darkened, and wandering from the fure guide, was pleafed to meet him in things more outward, to arreft his

attention,

attention, and make him fenfible of the offenfive-
nefs of his ftate and condition ; that fo, if it might
by any means be effected, he might turn to the
Lord, and find him a Saviour. Hence the law
entered with many very fignificant ceremonies
and fervices, pointing out man's need of purification, forgivenefs, and reftoration. All this was
to ferve as a " fchoolmafter to lead to Chrift."
It not only pointed to him as then yet to come a
great way off, or a long time hence ; but it
pointed to him alfo directly, as then at hand, in
and among them, if they would have known and
attended to him. For, fays Mofes (Deut. xxx.
11, &c.) " this commandment which I command thee this day, it is not hidden from thee,
neither is it far off. It is not in heaven, that thou
fhouldeft fay, who fhall go up for us to heaven,
and bring it untous, that we may hearit and do it?
neither is it beyond the fea, that thou fhouldeft
fay, who fhall go over the fea for us, and
bring it unto us, that we may hear it and do it?
but the word is very nigh thee, in thy mouth and
in thy heart, that thou mayeft do it. And verfe
20, he preffeth it upon them to love and cleave
unto the Lord, affuring them thus; " for he is
thy life, and the length of thy days."

Thus did Mofes point out the word near and in
them, and referred them plainly to the Lord
himfelf, as the life to their fouls. And Paul tells
the Romans, x. 8, that this word which Mofes
tells Ifrael was near and in them, " is the word of
faith, which we preach." And in the preceding
verfes exprefsly declares this to be the " righteoufnefs of faith;" and that it fpeaketh on this
wife, " fay not in thine heart, who fhall afcend
into

into heaven (that is, to bring Chriſt down from above) or who ſhall deſcend into the deep (that is, to bring Chriſt again from the dead,") &c. Hence it is clear, that the life of Chriſt the Lord near them and even in them, was what Moſes meant to point them to, and wiſh them to love and cleave unto, and which was nothing leſs than the true and living word of faith which the Apoſtles preached. This, as before hinted, has been the real life of all diſpenſations; and when and where the true reformation, return, and cleaving unto this, hearing and doing it, take place in purity and fulneſs, " all old things are paſſed away." The ſhadows vaniſh before the light, and the elements melt with the fervent heat of the goſpel ſun.

THESE things could never have been deſigned for perpetual continuance in the goſpel ſtate, but only to lead unto it. " For if that firſt covenant had been faultleſs, then ſhould no place have been ſought for the ſecond," Heb. viii. 7. John's baptiſm, as well as the paſſover, was under the firſt covenant, and no proper part of the ſecond. Had it been part of the ſecond, how could Chriſt have teſtified, as before noticed, that though among them that are born of women, there hath not riſen a greater than John the Baptiſt, notwithſtanding he that is leaſt in the kingdom of heaven is greater than he ? Mat. xi. 11: but the reaſon is now plain, as already evinced, why the leaſt in the kingdom of heaven is greater than he, to wit, that both he, as John the Baptiſt, and his baptiſm, belonged not to the ſecond covenant; and that therefore, as John the Baptiſt, he was but the adminiſtrator of a baptiſm that has no proper place

F

in

in Chriſt's ſpiritual kingdom, to the leaſt, in the purity of which, "all old things are paſſed away." This ſtate is evidently greater, as has been obſerved already, than that of John, as the baptizer in outward water, in which capacity he is here ſpoken of; and as ſuch he was to decreaſe, and his baptiſm to give place to Chriſt's.

As a ſaint and ſervant of God, he was never to decreaſe, but to "increaſe with the increaſe of God;" but his diſpenſation, his baptiſm, was ever deſigned to decreaſe, and be fulfilled. And I think it will be granted, that the leaſt in the pure kingdom of life and ſubſtance is, and muſt be, in the nature of things, greater than any ever could be in the mere adminiſtration of a decreaſing and terminating inſtitution.

JOHN was doubtleſs, as a Chriſtian (and ſuch there have been in all ages, Abraham was eminently one) great in the kingdom of heaven, but this was not as John the Baptiſt; as ſuch, he came to, but did not enter the kingdom, nor belong to it, he ſaw it with his eyes, and knew, and pointed to the Lord of it; but as Moſes went not over Jordan, though he did much towards leading Iſrael to their inheritance, but gave place to Joſhua, whoſe name, like that of Jeſus, ſignifies a Saviour, and who conducted them after Moſes into the good land; ſo John the Baptiſt, as ſuch, could not belong to the purely ſpiritual kingdom of our Lord; but gave place to him, the anointed Saviour, who baptizeth every member and ſubject of his church and kingdom, into the very life and power of the kingdom, which "is not meat and drink, but righteouſneſs, and peace, and joy

in the Holy Ghoft," Rom. xiv. 17. And feeing
John's baptifm was no part of the fecond covenant, but was under the firft, and its proper ufe
was only whilft the firft tabernacle was ftanding,
it is equally difannulled by the abolifhing of the
firft covenant, and removal of the firft tabernacle, with the other figurative obfervations;
and for the fame reafon was this difannulled, as
were the others, viz. its infufficiency, weaknefs,
and utter inability to make perfect the comers
thereunto. "For there is verily a difannulling
of the commandment, going before, for the weaknefs and unprofitablenefs thereof. For the law
made nothing perfect; but the bringing in of a
better hope did, by the which we draw nigh unto
God," Heb. vii. 18, 19. Here we fee that which
went before the new covenant ftate was, for its
weaknefs and unprofitablenefs in making perfect,
difannulled; and furely John's miniftration and
baptifm went before that ftate, and were defigned
exprefsly to prepare for it. I marvel that Chriftians do not fee it, and prefs on beyond it. It is
idle to fuppofe one fet of figns and ceremonies
difannulled for their weaknefs, and another fet
introduced as perpetual ordinances in the gofpel
ftate, we do not read, that, "finding fault" with
the rites, figures and ordinances of the firft
covenant; God ordained water-wafhing, and eating and drinking bread and wine, as more per-
manent and perpetual inftitutions of the new
or fecond covenant. Nay, verily, he finds fault
equally with all things in their own nature equally
partaking of the fame weaknefs; both were of
divine inftitution for a time, and equally weak
and liable to a neceffary abrogation; and being
both typical, there was no more perpetual per-

F 2   manency

manency in the one than the other; neither in themfelves, nor in their inftitution, and of the Mofaic inftitutions, it is exprefsly faid, finding fault with them, he faith, "behold the days come, faith the Lord, when 1 will make a new covenant with the houfe of Ifrael, and with the houfe of Judah," Heb. viii. 8. Now what was this new covenant ? It was intended to fupercede and fupply the defects of the old ; but there is not one word of any of thofe outward ordinances in it.—They are all old things ; and however extolled by many good men, belong to the old covenant forever. So that the ceremonials of the law are as much gofpel ordinances as water baptifm, or bread and wine.

THE new covenant is altogether inward and fpiritual. "For this is the covenant that I will make with the houfe of Ifrael, after thofe days, faith the Lord; 1 will put my laws into their mind, and write them in their hearts, and I will be to them a God, and they fhall be to me a people," &c. verfe 10. "Chrift has not entered into the holy places, made with hands, which are the figures of the true," Heb. ix. 24. Nor ought we, if we would become completely his followers, to continue in the figurative wafhings, any more than in the figurative offerings and old ceremonious worfhip of that temple, which was but a figure of the true.—" The priefthood being changed, there is made of neceffity a change alfo of the law," vii. 12. It behoved that the baptifms accompanying the firft priefthood, the worldly tabernacle, and holy places made with hands, fhould, like them, be outward : but now, the law being changed, and the covenant written in the heart, a fpiritual baptifm alone can be proper, and

and accordingly is the one only baptifm of the gofpel, for if it was neceffary "that the patterns of the heavenly things," thefe being outward, fhould be figuratively purified with outward fprinklings, wafhings, &c. furely it is as necef-fary that the heavenly things themfelves be puri-fied with better facrifices and wafhings than thefe." See Heb. ix. 23. I think if the vail were done away in the experience of Chriftians, they might in this one text, Heb. x. 5, " when he cometh into the world, he faith, facrifice and offerings thou wouldeft not, but a body haft thou prepared me," read clearly the difmiffion of all figurative atonements and purifications ; all the facrifices and offerings "he taketh away"—as the firft things, "that he may eftablifh the fecond"—that is, " lo I come to do thy will, O God." This muft be done in all the feed; and this is the thing that remaineth forever, eftablifhed under the gofpel.—The fcope of the Apoftle's reafoning in this chapter, againft the continuation of the " fhadows of the good things to come," is from their weaknefs, their impro-priety and ufeleffnefs, where the fubftance is known, and thus he argues, that where remiffion of fins is obtained, there is no more offering for fin. See verfe 18. Why then continue a baptifm that was exprefsly unto repentance, for the remif-fion of fins, if we have obtained remiffion ? Paul brings in the new covenant written in the heart, and the remiffion of fins, attending it. " Their fins and iniquities will I remember no more ;" and in the very next words forms the above conclufion. Now where remiffion of thefe is, there is no more offering for fin.—And after he gets through with the argument, inftead of urging any outward bap-

F 3

tifms,

tifms, or figurative obfervations, he preffingly
enjoins love, good works, holding faft, not drawing back, not neglecting affembling, not to caft
away confidence, patience, &c.—Can any thing
be plainer, than that fuch care and conftancy in
faith, patience, and godly walking, according to
the writing of the new covenant, are the weighty
matters of the gofpel difpenfation in Paul's
eftimation? that as he was not fent to baptize
with water, fo he never in all his writing enjoins
it, nor reproves for its omiffion; he fpeaks of
the believers, not as being then exercifed in the
terrible things at Sinai, but as come to the excellent things of Mount Sion, "the heavenly Jerufalem, to the fpirits of juft men made perfect;
and to Jefus the mediator of the new covenant; to
the blood of fprinkling," &c. This is all fufficient without the figures—and fo he fhows the removal of all elfe, "Yet once more I fhake not
the earth only; but alfo heaven"—this is the removal of things that are fhaken—"that thofe
things which cannot be fhaken may remain."
"Wherefore" (fays he) "we receiving a kingdom which cannot be moved, let us have grace,
whereby we may ferve God acceptably with re-
verence and godly fear." See about the latter
half of chapter xii. and xiii. 9. He fubjoins
"be not carried about with divers and ftrange
doctrines; for it is a good thing that the heart be
eftablifhed with grace; not with meats which
have not profited them that have been occupied
therein."—Did he not mean thefe elementary
things, by the ftrange doctrines? if not, why
does he fo immediately propofe grace as the means
of eftablifhment, and difcountenance meats as
unprofitable? and what means the altar in the next
verfe,

verfe, whereof they have no right to eat which
ferve the tabernacle? is not this altar and that
which is eaten, by the we, who have it, and
have a right to eat of it, fomething belonging to the kingdom they have received which
cannot be fhaken? and are not the meats,
drinkings and wafhings, that are unprofitable,
the things that are fhaken? and why is the
fhaking and removal of thefe, called fhaking
heaven? is it not plainly becaufe thefe are things
that had pertained to devotion and religious
fervices, and were yet urged as fuch by too
many? and can any thing remain of a ceremonial
nature, where this heaven is thoroughly fhaken,
where all old things are done away, and all things
become new, according to the new and living
way of the gofpel?—This epiftle is fuppofed to
have been written in the year fixty-four; fo
that there had been a pretty full time of trial
what was and what was not profitable to thofe
who had been occupied in them; and we find
here many good things inculcated and enjoined;
but ceremonials are rejected, as pertaining to
the firft covenant, and as now fhaken and removed; and is it not truly worthy of remark, that
John, the beloved difciple of our Lord, who
is fuppofed to have written his hiftory of Chrift's
life and doctrines many years after his afcenfion, makes no mention at all of our Saviour's
conduct at the eating of the paffover, in regard
to the difciples eating and drinking in remembrance of him—but relates very circumftanti-
ally his other conduct of wafhing the difciples
feet, and the inftructive leffon couched in it?

MAY we not fairly conclude, that as the only

propee

proper time of the difciples' eating and drinking in remembrance of Chrift, was but until
his coming again, the Comforter to take up
his abode with them, and lead and guide them
into all truth; and as this feafon was long
elapfed, when John wrote, that therefore, he
thinking it of no ufe to mention it, paffed
it in total filence, as one of the many things
which Jefus truly did, but which are not noticed.
in his hiftory? We find him very careful in
correcting a hearfay report, which might, if believed, tend to lead people into outward obfervances, which he appears not to have relied
on, nor inculcated in all his writings. The
report I allude to is that, by the fpreading
whereof "the Pharifees had heard that Jefus
made and baptized more difciples than John"
the Baptift. This miftake the beloved difciple,
who leaned on Jefus' bofom, and having near
accefs to his heart, knew much of his mind
and will, takes fpecial care to rectify, by a
full declaration that "Jefus himfelf baptized
not, but his difciples." Obferving this general
omiffion of things not effential, and his great
care to tranfmit down to pofterity many heavenly
and truly evangelical and deeply interefting
fayings, exhortations and divine intimations of
the bleffed Jefus; I have been ready to fuppofe
his whole aim, in mentioning water baptifm at
all, was juft to do John the Baptift and the
Pharifees juftice; properly introduce Jefus as
increafing, and John as decreafing; carefully
record John's repeated mention of water, as
peculiar to his baptifm, in direct contradiftinction to Chrift's; and pointedly to contradict
the

the miſtaken opinion, that Chriſt baptized in
water.

John knew very well the diſciples did ſo, and
doubtleſs knew on what ground it was. Let any
one read carefully his evangelical hiſtory and
epiſtles, and obſerve his almoſt total ſilence
about many things related by others, and how
he abounds in the mention of deep ſpiritual
matters; and ſee if it does not greatly favour the
opinion, that John ſaw the abundant need of
preſerving and inculcating things of an inward,
living, ſpiritual import and concernment, and
divine nature: he aimed at life and ſubſtance,
and carefully retained what is moſt livingly
expreſſive of it, and what tends moſt immediately to promote the knowledge of it among
men. In his epiſtles he dwells almoſt entirely on
things really eſſential: he makes the old commandment, the word they had "heard from the
beginning"—and the new, "which thing" (ſays
he) "is true in him and in you," to centre in the
doctrine of the true light that now ſhineth, 1
John ii. 7, 8. And his advices are to faithful-
neſs in keeping and abiding in the holy word,
to love and good works; but not a word of exhortation to ceremonials.—And may we not fairly
conclude, both water baptiſm, and the bread and
wine, were much laid aſide, or very little relied
upon or inculcated, at the late period at which
this beloved diſciple wrote?

CHAP

C H A P. IV.

Christ's baptism is into *the* name, *i. e. life and* power *of the Godhead. So his commission to his disciples to administer it, could not be executed but by divine power. They waiting for, received* this, *and baptized others with it. All gospel preaching is herein, and in its nature. is baptizing. Christ's baptism effects* entire *sanctification. John's a lively* type *of it, being* all over *in water. It shewed the need of cleansing and remission, but effected neither. Christ's alone can. John constantly distinguishes* his *from Christ's, by the word* water. *Christ baptized none in water, nor ordered it (that appears) but doubtless would, had it been his baptism. None of the prophecies point him out so baptizing, but as effecting inward changes. Disciples use of water no more perpetuates it, than their use of circumcision, anointing with oil, vows, &c. do them. Paul's commission full, yet he thanks God he baptized so few. Council at Jerusalem did not advise water, bread or wine.*

LET us now attend more particularly to the great baptismal commission, Mat. 28. The 18th verse introduceth it thus: " and Jesus came

came and fpake unto them, faying, all power is given unto me in heaven and in earth." A very proper introduction to command attention, in-fpire confidence, and fhow them whence their whole qualification to teach baptizingly was to proceed. 19th, "Go ye therefore and teach all nations, baptizing them *eis to onoma*, into the name of the Father, and of the Son, and of the Holy Ghoft." 20th, " Teaching them to obferve all things whatfoever I have commanded you: and lo! I am with you alway, even unto the end of the world. Amen." Obferve he fays, "go ye therefore;" that is, becaufe "I have all pow-er," and can and will qualify you fo to teach, in my own life and power, as thereby to baptize the people into the very name, the power, virtue and life, of the Divinity. Obferve further, the commiffion is not teach, and baptize, as two dif-tinct acts; but teach, baptizing. And, as fuch a work might feem almoft too great for their faith, he adds, that he (who had all power) would be with them in the work, and that to the end of the world.

It is plain that this commiffion, as it enjoins a very fpecial kind of teaching, fuch as fhould bap-tize the people into true difciplefhip, as members of the body, the church of Chrift; fo it could not be executed but by a fupernatural affiftance received from on high. " Behold" (faid Chrift) " I fend the promife of my Father upon you; but tarry ye in the city of Jerufalem, until ye be endued with power from on high," Luke xxiv. 49. John truly baptized with water, but ye fhall be baptized with the Holy Ghoft not many days hence," Acts i. v. " Ye fhall receive power after that

that the Holy Ghoft is come upon you; and ye
fhall be witnefles unto me, both in Jerufalem,
and in all Judea, and in Samaria, and unto the
uttermoft part of the earth," verfe 8. Thus evident it is, that their being living witnefles of
Chrift depended on the power of the Holy Ghoft
coming upon them; and that they could never
adminifter his baptifm, till they were thereby fo
endued, as to teach, baptizing into the fame
Spirit themfelves were baptized with. This baptifm into the name, they in due time fo eminently
received, as they waited for it according to direction—" with one accord in one place," Acts
ii. 1; that is probably in filent retirement, waiting upon God; that in the power thereof they
taught with fuch baptizing efficacy, that multitudes were pricked in their heart, Acts ii. 37.
The Holy Ghoft fell on them which heard the
word, chap. x. 44. Their very enemies were not
able to refift the wifdom and the fpirit by which
they fpake, as chap. vi. 10. Thus truly "with
great power gave the Apoftles witnefs of the refurrection of the Lord Jefus," chap. iv. 33. And
thus they preached the gofpel unto the people,
" with the Holy Ghoft fent down from heaven,"
1 Peter i. 12. No wonder then it fell on thofe who
in true faith, that was of the operation of God,
received the word, and gladly embraced the gofpel. Chrift promifed, " he that believeth on me,
as the fcripture hath faid, out of his belly fhall
flow rivers of living water; but this fpake he of
the Spirit, which they that believe on him fhould
receive," John vii. 38, 39. And what can be
more natural than for it to flow into others, as it
flows out of them? efpecially as Chrift's exprefs
direction was, " freely ye have received, freely
give."

give." It seems the Spirit not only flows into, and continues to flow in the hearts of true believers, but more or less flows out of them upon others; for they are, as Chrift teftifies, the "light of the world," Mat. v. 14; "the falt of the earth," 13; "a city fet upon an hill," 14, &c. He promifed to make his difciples "fifhers of men."

Some affirm, no man can baptize with the Holy Ghoft, truly none can, in his own time and ability; nor can any preach the gofpel but by divine affiftance. All true gofpel miniftry is in the life of the Son of God, and wherever it proves effectual to the converfion of fouls, it is a baptizing miniftry. None are fifhers of men, but who are made fo by Chrift : learning and eloquence may amufe, but it is the Holy Ghoft fent down from heaven that makes gofpel preachers. This fheds itfelf through fuch, in a bleffed diffufion upon others, oft times, in a very lively, inftruftive and foul-benefiting manner. And this is a thing as experimentally known, where the real gofpel, which is the power of God unto falvation, is preached in the life, evidence and demonftration of the Spirit, and with power, as any gofpel experience whatever; and it is ftrange to hear Chriftians deny it.

Does the preaching of the gofpel in our day fucceed or not to the real benefit of fouls? If not, it is ufelefs. If it does, what caufes the benefit? Is it of God, or of man? Art thou fo vain, oh! man, as to think thou canft do any fpiritual good of thyfelf, unaffifted by the Spirit of Chrift? If this is thy idea, thou art no true

gofpel

gospel minister; for they know they can do nothing of themselves.—If thou art sensible of the help, life and assistance of the holy Spirit in thy ministry, and of a divine and beneficial influence on the minds of those who partake of it, thou mayst rest assured, that so far as it is truly so, it is through the operation of the Holy Ghost on their hearts; and whatever be the degree of this, more or less, thy ministry is so far, and no further, a baptizing ministry: so far, and no further, it is truly the ministry of the gospel. And it is thus, and only thus, that it pleaseth "God, through the foolishness of preaching, to save them that believe," 1 Cor. i. 21.—It is very unlikely that any should be saved through preaching, unless thereby baptized with the one saving baptism, for nothing else ever can save. Hence, clear it is, that through true gospel preaching, this baptism is administered to them that believe; the word preached being mixed with faith in them that hear it. And no ministry that is not in its own nature, life and influence, baptizing, is in any degree the genuine ministry of the gospel.—But, thanks be unto God, there is yet preserved a living, powerful and heart-baptizing ministry; and many are the living witnesses of it, and of its blessed effects; and I am well confirmed, that no rightly qualified gospel minister can doubt of the baptizing influence of right ministry. He who knows Christ, living, acting and speaking in him, knows that which alone baptizes with the Holy Ghost and with fire. "I in them, and thou in me," says Christ to his Father, John xvii. 23. And many other texts declare Christ in us; and true and blessed experience indubitably confirms it. What then can

be

be too hard for his minifters, in and under his influence? Paul fays, "I can do all things through Chrift, which ftrengtheneth me," Phil. iv. 13. But Chrift himfelf puts the matter beyond all reafonable difpute, John xiv. 12; and he afferts it with "a verily, verily, I fay unto you, he that believeth on me, the works that I do fhall he do; and greater works than thefe fhall he do; becaufe I go to my Father." Hence Paul fays, "I have begotten you, through the gofpel," 1 Cor. iv. 15; and fpeaks of imparting fpiritual gifts, Rom. i. 11. Hence, on the laying on of the Apoftles hands, "the Holy Ghoft was given," Acts viii. 18. Hence, as Peter began to fpeak to the houfhold of Cornelius, the Holy Ghoft fell on them. And hence Chrift fays (in confideration that it was he who fpake in his difciples, and his Father in him, and fo in them) "he that receiveth you, receiveth me; and he that receiveth me, receiveth him that fent me," Mat. x. 40. On this ground Paul calls himfelf "the minifter of Jefus Chrift to the Gentiles; miniftering the gofpel of God, that the offering up of the Gentiles might be acceptable, being fanctified by the Holy Ghoft," Rom. xv. 16. And verfe 18 he adds, "for I will not dare to fpeak of any of thefe things, which Chrift hath not wrought by me." Well then might he fpeak of miniftering the gofpel, which is the power of God; feeing it was all the work of Chrift by him, and refulted in fanctification, by the Holy Ghoft, the baptizing power of the gofpel. Indeed the very defign of the gofpel miniftry is to open people's eyes, and to turn them from darknefs to light, and from the power of Satan unto God," Acts xxvi. 18.

THIS

THIS miniftry lays the axe to the root of the corrupt trees in men's hearts, and therein is executing the very work of Chrift. It is truly Chrift that does the work; but he works much by inftruments: John was a great inftrument in his hand: his miniftry was very ufeful in helping to kindle that fire which was to burn up the chaff. He powerfully taught the neceffity of this fiery baptifm, and of renouncing all dependence on being Abraham's children. This was a good beginning, and was a very neceffary preparation for Chrift, who had afterwards ftill further, and preffingly too, to combat and alarm that difpofition, perhaps as prevalent now as at that day; and that among too many profeffing Chriftians, may I not fay, of all denominations? I belong to this or that reformed and truly religious fociety; we are in the true faith and practice of the Apoftles. Here thoufands ftick in a lifelefs profeffion, as to themfelves; and yet imagine themfelves the true feed and offspring of Abraham, fpiritually. And it is very hard removing them from their ftrong holds, or making them fenfible of the need of the axe and the fire. John's miniftry was to fuch, doubtlefs, truly awakening. And then, as already obferved, his dipping them, not partly, but all over in water, was a lively and very ftriking reprefentation of the baptifm whereby Chrift thoroughly cleanfeth the floor of the heart. And to point out this, and to enkindle a defire to experience it, was all that outward dipping could do, fave to wafh away the outward filth of the flefh. It could do nothing in itfelf towards real remiffion of fins; that is the work of Chrift, and the foul is brought to experience it through his baptifm. Hence John was very careful to prevent
the

the idea of his own baptifm being faving., He
never once fpeaks of it, that I recollect, but he
adds the word water, to turn the mind from refting in it, as a thing in any wife profitable, further
than as it reprefented a perfect cleanfing and purification by Chrift's, and engaged them to prefs
after it. I indeed baptize you with water, but
Chrift fhall baptize you with the Holy Ghoft
and fire, and thereby cleanfe you thoroughly
within, as I wafh, or dip you all over outwardly,
is the import of John's teftimony. And three
times, in eight verfes, fpeaking of his own baptifm, he every time carefully adds the word watei,
in contradiftinction to Chrift's. Firft, being examined why he baptized, if he was not Chrift,
Elias, nor that prophet; it feems he thought it
apology enough to tell them, John i. 26, " I
baptize with water ;" and refer them to Chrift for
gofpel baptifm, that is of the Holy Ghoft. For
outward water being no part of Chrift's baptifm,
but being long before then in fome fort practifed
among the Jews, it was no intrufion into Chrift's
office for John to baptize with it. So that this
fhort anfwer of John, that he only baptized with
water (an old practice) an outward, and comparatively a low thing, entirely different from
Chrift's baptifm, and no part of it, was amply
fufficient to exculpate John from any juft imputation of meddling with things too high for him,
or belonging to another. But further to evince
how careful John was to keep up the diftinction
that forever exifts, in the very ground and nature
of them, between his baptifm and Chrift's—we
find that in the 31ft verfe he again dwells on or
repeats this important diftinction, by the word
water, " that he fhould be made manifeft to
                    G   Ifrael,

Ifrael, therefore am I come baptizing with water"
—and no further on than the next verfe but one,
the 33d, he again holds up the fame diftinction;
" he that fent me to baptize with water, the fame
faid unto me, upon whom thou fhalt fee the
Spirit defcending and remaining on him, the fame
is he which baptizeth with the Holy Ghoft."—
One would think this three-fold teftimony, all
in fo fhort a time, might fatisfy every fober mind
that water baptifm, and that of Chrift, are entirely two diftinct and feparate things; and more
efpecially, as touching water, it is very particularly recorded that Jefus himfelf baptized not. He
might and did, with a great deal of wifdom and
condefcending goodnefs, as noted before, allow
his difciples to do it, in that weak and early ftate
and ftage of things, before all the fhadows could
well be laid afide, their minds not being then
able to bear it: " I have yet many things to fay
unto you, but ye cannot bear them now," John
xvi. 12. And as the difciples did, through this all-
wife permiffion, baptize confiderable numbers, and
that upon their faith in and following Jefus, and
becoming his difciples, it was but natural for the
people to confider it as if Chrift had done it himfelf. Nor is it at all ftrange therefore that " the
pharifees had heard that Jefus made and baptized
more difciples than John (though Jefus himfelf
baptized not, but his difciples") John iv. 1, 2.
And as what a man does by others, he is often
called the doer of; fo the people then (fuppofing
the difciples baptized by Chrift's authority and
commiffion, becaufe they were his difciples and
followers whom they fo baptized) faid he baptized; but it is clear enough that he only fuffered
it, and that in condefcenfion; nor do I believe it
would

would ever have been so carefully recorded that
he himself baptized not, had outward water been
any part of his baptism; but his baptism being
quite another thing, he saw it proper wholly to
avoid administering outward water as an ordinance; and that probably left it should counte-
nance an idea that it belonged to his gospel and
kingdom; and so strengthen the already too strong
attachment of the people to things outward; and
to prevent this in after times, it was also proper,
that it should be expresly recorded that "Jesus
himself baptized not; and in confirmation of these
sentiments it may be observed, that he never once
on any occasion enjoined it on any to baptize, or
be baptized, in water—we read particularly what
he did, and what he ordered done, on divers particular occasions.—Many believed on him, many
he healed, and cast out devils; but never a word
that he either baptized any of these, or ordered
them baptized, in water.—We read expresly, that
he directed one to go and offer for his cleansing
"the gift that Moses commanded, for a testi-
mony unto them," Mat. viii. 4. Another he
ordered to "go wash in the pool of Siloam," John
ix. 7: but not an instance of any one ordered by
him to be baptized by another in water. But
had water baptism been his, or any part of his
gospel, it would have been a strange thing indeed
had he never vouchsafed once to administer it,
nor order it done on any of the multitudes that
believed on him, or out of whom he cast devils,
or whom he healed. And even this omission
alone, it prevailing throughout the whole history
of his life, both before and after his resurrection,
were in my view sufficient to overthrow the
notion

notion of water baptifm being a gofpel ordinance.

WHAT! appoint a folemn ordinance, even a
facrament (as fome call it) of perpetual obligation in the church, and never once deign to adminifter it, or order it adminiftered to any indi-
vidual, among all the thoufands who became his
difciples ? This were ftrange indeed; and to me
is quite incredible, and inadmiffible. Indeed
among all the very pointed and remarkable prophecies concerning Chrift, there is not one in
all the Old Teftament that points him out as the
adminiftrator of water baptifm, or as eftablifhing
a church or kingdom accompanied with any fuch
outward ordinances. The Father, by Ifaiah,
fpeaks of him as the Lord's Elect, in whom his
foul delighteth; declaring, If. xlii. 1, "I have
put my Spirit upon him"—giving him "for a
covenant to the people, for a light to the Gentiles, to open blind eyes, to bring out the pri-
foners, and them that fit in darknefs," &c. and
further, "behold the former things are come to
pafs, and new things do I declare; before they
fpring forth, I tell you of them." But not a
word, among all thefe new things, of his baptizing in outward water. His work was to bring
forth judgment unto truth, enlighten the Gentiles, bring out of prifon and darknefs, "bring
the blind by a way they knew not," an inward
fpiritual way; not the way of figns, fhadows, and
outward ordinances—thefe were the old things;
"I will lead them in paths that they have not
known." Thefe are inward.

AGAIN, If. lii. 13, "Behold my fervant fhall
deal prudently," &c.—15. "fo fhall he fprinkle
many.

many nations," &c. He was indeed more truly
wife and prudent, than to practife or efteem outward fprinkling or dipping as a gofpel ordinance;
his is a fpiritual fprinkling, as explained Ez.
xxxvi. 25, "then will I fprinkle clean water
upon you, and ye fhall be clean." The 26th and
27th verfes promife a new heart, and new fpirit—
the Lord's Spirit put within them. Such things
as thefe did the prophets foretel—but not once
in all their predictions, of return, reformation,
reftoration, and building the wafte places, and
the like, do they ever mention or hint at Chrift's
baptizing with water, or eftablifhing any fuch
kind of fhadowy inftitutions in his glorious gofpel
church. Nor did Chrift, when he came, ever
once, that we read of, call that of water his baptifm. Indeed it is never once fo called in all the
Bible, that I can find. And, moreover, I do not
find that Chrift ever called it by any other name.
than John's baptifm. And is it not wonderful,
that he fhould conftantly, and as often as he fpake
of water baptifm, call it John's, if it was as truly
his own, as John's? Or how can we fuppofe he
ordained it as a ftanding ordinance in his church,
and yet never mentioned it once as fuch?—Why
fhould he leave his followers, to the world's end,
under the great difficulties and difadvantages of
fuch a total filence, if he willed them to ufe it as
his baptifm? Was Mofes more faithful in his
houfe, than Chrift in his? Mofes was very particular in defcribing the rituals of the law, even to
very minute circumftances: and would Chrift
ordain a perpetual inftitution, and never once
call it his own, but always call it John's? He
knew very well that both himfelf, John, and
others, called and underftood water baptifm to

G 3   be

be John's. He alfo knew his own was repeatedly placed in direct contradiftinction to it—and faid to be with the Holy Ghoft. So that in commiffion-ating his difciples to adminifter his own baptifm, there was no need to defcribe it over again ; for it had been fo often exprefsly defined, and dif-tinguifhed from that of water, that he might well fuppofe no real difciple of his need be at a lofs to know what he meant by the word baptizing in his great gofpel commiffion—and efpecially after having fo abundantly, and on fo many occafions, taught them the inward and fpiritual nature of his kingdom, and fo repeatedly turned their minds from outward obfervations, to inward realities.

But had he inftituted water baptifm, after all this, as a gofpel ordinance, it would have been highly requifite for him to have expreffed it to be water, in the moft particular manner—much more fo than if his baptifm had never been named as different from water. He might well know his followers would be apt to conclude he infti-tuted his own baptifm, and not one which had fo repeatedly been exprefsly diftinguifhed there-from. He might well know that thofe whofe minds were, at leaft in degree, opened by his repeated endeavours to turn them from things outward to things inward, from figns to fub-ftance, would not be unlikely to underftand his words to mean fpiritually; inftead of turning back, to fuppofe him now at laft bringing them in bondage to weak and beggarly elements. He had comforted their forrowful fouls with a pro-mife of coming again to them in fpirit, and taking up his abode with them, and thus remaining with them to the end of the world.—Almoft every thing

thing he had faid to them, for fome time paft, had tended directly and indeed been by him de-figned, to lead inward, and to a fpiritual dif-cerning and underftanding of things; fo that had he now, juft before he left them, turned back, and in direct contradiction to the very nature of his gofpel and kingdom, and to the whole fcope and tenor of his own excellent parables and dif-courfes, inftituted an outward baptifm or fupper, it might furely be expected he would have told them exprefsly what he intended—nor can I fup-pofe he would by any means have omitted it.— I am fo well affured of the fpirituality of the gofpel, and of Chrift's doctrines and difcourfes, that I cannot entertain the leaft idea, but that had he eftablifhed outward figns, he would have very explicitly declared them to be outward.—Others may think otherwife. But though I have great charity and good-will for many who adhere to thofe figns, I cannot but think, that where they come to have a full view of the purity of the gofpel ftate, and a clear underftanding of the drift and defign of Chrift's many hints, intima-tions, and heavenly communications to his dif-ciples, they muft fee the total abolition of all the mere rituals, both of John and of Mofes.

It is often urged, that Chrift's difciples bap-tized in water. I conceive this no more per-petuates water baptifm, than their circumcifing, purifying, fhaving, vows, anointing the fick with oil, abftaining from blood, and from things ftrangled, perpetuate thefe things in the church. —Thefe two laft were exprefsly enjoined by the elders, even upon the Gentiles, and that after deliberate confideration and debate, at the time

of

of the great Council at Jerufalem, Acts 15, though
at the fume time, through affiftance of the Holy
Ghoft, they decreed against circumcifing the
Gentiles, and confidered circumcifion as an uneafy
yoke; yet in the beginning of the very next
chapter, we read that Paul, though he and Timothy had thefe very decrees to deliver, to be
kept as they paffed through the cities, even at
fuch a juncture as this, he acted fo greatly in
condefcenfion to the weaknefs of the Jews, that
he circumcifed Timothy, becaufe of them; and
after he had paffed on, and they had delivered
faid decrees, on his return again to Jerufalem,
all the elders, with James (who had pointedly
decided againft circumcifion in regard to the
Gentiles) told Paul that many thoufands of the
Jews believed; that they were zealous of circumcifion and the law of Mofes, and advifed him to
purify himfelf, and be at charges, &c. with four
men that had a vow; that fo thofe over-zealous
Jews might fee he kept the law, and walked
orderly, Acts, xxi. 20—24.—And yet in the next
verfe they fay, "as touching the Gentiles which
believe, we have written and concluded that they
obferve no fuch thing," &c. So we read, ver. 26,
"then Paul took the men, and the next day
purifying himfelf with them, entered into the
temple, to fignify the accomplifhment of the
days of purification, until that an offering fhould
be offered for every one of them." So very great
was the condefcenfion of the primitive Apoftles
and elders to the weak ftate of the people in thofe
early times.—To the weak, Paul fays he became
weak, yea that he was made all things to all men,
that he might fave fome, 1 Cor. ix. 22; and this
he exprefsly declares he did for the gofpel fake,

verfe

verſe 25.—Yea further he ſays expreſsly, he caught them with guile, 2 Cor. xii. 16. This kind of condeſcending guile they doubtleſs thought neceſſary in thoſe times of weakneſs and zeal for ordinances.—Paul's knowledge of Chriſt was by revelation, and ſo he ſaw clearly beyond thoſe outſide things, and knew that neither they, nor water baptiſm, could poſſibly belong to the goſpel. Hence, though on the ſame principle of condeſcenſion he baptized a few, he thanked God it was ſo very few; and declared he was not ſent commiſſioned to do it, 1 Cor. i. 17. Had he not known it was not Chriſt's baptiſm, nor within the great commiſſion, he would not have dared to affront his Lord, by thanking him that he had ſo almoſt totally neglected his great goſpel ordinance.—Paul's commiſſion to the Gentiles, Acts xxvi. 18, is expreſsly " to open their eyes, and to turn them from darkneſs to light, and from the power of Satan unto God, that they may receive forgiveneſs of ſins, and inheritance among them which are ſanctified, by faith that is in me." This is as full, and contains the very ſum and eſſence of the general commiſſion, Mat. xxviii. 19, &c. and Mark xvi. only that it ſeems confined to the Gentiles.

THE general commiſſion is, to teach all nations, baptizing them into the name, &c. and declares that he that believeth, and is ſo baptized, ſhall be ſaved.—Paul's commiſſion is to open the eyes of the Gentiles, and turn them from darkneſs to the light, and from the power of Satan to God. And if any can doubt whether this is the ſame baptizing miniſtry of the goſpel, mentioned in the more general commiſſion, let the concluding words of Paul's commiſſion be duly weighed, "that

" that they may receive forgivenefs of fins, and inheritance among them which are fanctified, by faith that is in me."—Here they were not only to receive forgivenefs of fins, but the fame inheritance with all the other fanctified, and that through the fame faith; for thus believing, they were baptized through the powerful miniftry of the Apoftle, which was in the evidence and demonftration of the Spirit, &c. into the life, power and virtue of the fame eternal name: they were turned truly unto God; and thus truly believing, and being livingly and fanctifyingly baptized into the fame holy name, and into the fame heavenly inheritance, and therein abiding, the promife that they fhall be faved, was equally in force to them, as to others fo believing and being fo baptized: that if there is any effential difference in thefe two commiffions, as to what was to be done by thofe fent forth in the execution of them, I have not yet difcovered it, except in Paul's limitation to the Gentiles; and I have not the leaft doubt but that Paul did, in the execution of this commiffion, as truly baptize into the name of the Father, Son and Holy Ghoft, as ever an Apoftle of Chrift did, under the general commiffion; yea, did adminifter the very fame baptifm therein enjoined, that is Chrift's, and not John's. I am full in the faith, that Paul well knew the general commiffion contained no precept for water baptifm. He knew too well the nature and fpirituality of Chrift's kingdom, to fuppofe it did—and therefore doing what he did, at baptizing with water, in mere condefcenfion, he might as well, when he faw the abufe made of it, thank God that he had done no more—as he might that he had circumcifed no more; for as neither circumcifion

cifion nor uncircumcifion, fimply, is any thing
in this kingdom; fo neither is baptifm nor non-
baptifm in water, fimply, any thing at all therein—but the new creature: and this is all in all in
this fpiritual kingdom.

SOME may think I make very bold with gofpel
ordinances, as they call them; but though I feel
tendernefs towards many who think them fuch, I
am at no lofs in pronouncing them no real parts
of the gofpel. And if they had been, why did
not the great Council at Jerufalem, when it feemed
good to the Holy Ghoft and to them to lay upon
the Gentiles no greater burthen than the few
things they then named, mention water baptifm,
and the bread and wine, as things neceffary to be
punctually obferved? Paul was in that Council:
and he knew water baptifm was defigned that
Chrift " might be made manifeft to Ifrael"—and
did not wifh the Gentiles burthened with it, any
more than with circumcifion. He and others, as
occafion might feem to require, in becoming all
things to all men, in thofe early times of weaknefs and mifguided zeal for externals, might condefcend to baptize either a Jew or a Gentile: but
neither the one nor the other could any more be
brought under this fign, as a gofpel ordinance,
than under the many figns and fymbols of the
Mofaic law. I could go through every inftance
recorded in fcripture, where it was ufed by the
Apoftles, and I think clearly evince, that in no
one cafe it was ufed as ftrictly pertaining to the
kingdom of the Meffiah, nor under or according
to his great gofpel commiffion: but fo much of
this kind has been done by others, as, Dell, Bar-
clay, Penn, Pike, Claridge, Forfter, Phipps, Fo-
thergill, &c. that I think it not neceffary to be

fo

fo particular; firmly believing, that when men lay afide all preconceived opinions, and look fully and fairly into the nature and defign of the gofpel, in the true light and life of it, they muft unavoidably fee all thefe "old things done away;" and perceive how earneft Paul in particular was, to prevent the believers from degenerating into an attachment to and reliance on things outward. Read the whole epiftle to the Galatians; it abounds with his care on this account. And if we go to the bottom of things, we fhall find the fame need of preffing forward to the difufe of water baptifm, as of other ceremonials. It is as mere a ceremony, as merely figurative, as was circumcifion, or any of the divers wafhings; has no more in its nature or effects to fupport its continuance; and is no more perpetuated among the precepts and injunctions of Jefus.

CHAP.

C H A P. V.

Remarks on several passages in "A plain Account of the Ordinance of Baptism" (as the author calls it.) He is or was a sensible writer; but striving to unite old shadows with the gospel, he, like all who attempt it, blunders. Christ takes the lambs in his bosom, and bears with much weakness. The vail is done away in Christ. He is the end of all things. His are not subject to ordinances, in things that perish with the using. If all waited God's sending, water baptism, &c. would cease, and preaching would all be in baptizing efficacy. The non-experience of this, a cause of doubt in many, whether gospel-ministry is baptizing. Christ's ministers not always ready, but minister the Spirit to others, as it is given them. The words " into the name of the Father," &c., not a form to use in so low an act as that of water baptism. Hence never once so used by the Primitives; but, doubtless would have been, had water been the baptism of the commission. Peter's commanding baptism at Cornelius', no more perpetuates it, than Paul's baptizing Crispus and Gaius, though not sent to do it; nor any more than the use of circumcision, purifying, anointing with oil, &c. perpetuate them. The name, is the virtue, power, &c. Christ Lord of the Sabbath-day —and of all figurative institutions made under the law, to redeem those under it. Then John was under it, so his baptism ended. It was in some
sort

fort ufed under the law, long before John. Old rituals not to be incorporated into Chrift's pure religion and worfhip. His talk with the woman of Samaria, and with John's difciples, import this. His faft is inward.

IT is remarkable how ftrongly the advocates for dipping or plunging infift, in their arguings againft the Pædo Baptifts, or fuch as fprinkle infants, upon a plain, full and exprefs command. This I think they pretty generally maintain to be neceffary. The author of " A plain account of the ordinance of baptifm," as he calls it, and who feems to be as fenfible a writer as almoft any I have read in defence of water baptifm by immerfion, maintains thefe propofitions, page 4, Bofton edition.

" I. THE receiving of baptifm is not a duty of itfelf, or a duty apparent to us from the nature of things; but a duty, made fuch to Chriftians by the pofitive inftitution of Jefus Chrift.

" II. ALL pofitive duties, or duties made fuch by inftitution alone, depend entirely upon the will and declaration of the perfon who inftitutes or ordains them, with refpect to the real defign and end of them; and confequently to the due manner of performing them.

" III. IT is plain, therefore, that the nature, the defign, and the due manner of receiving baptifm, muft of neceffity depend upon what Jefus Chrift, who inftituted it, hath declared about it."

On

ON which I would remark, that if the nature, end and defign, with the due manner of adminiftring and receiving Chrift's baptifm, muft depend entirely upon what he himfelf hath declared about it, I think it is plain, that the nature of it is altogether inward and fpiritual. He never once calls outward baptifm with water his; never once declares any fuch thing about his, as that elementary water or any other outward thing belongs to it; but diftinguifhing his own from that of water, fays plainly, " John truly baptized with water, but ye fhall be baptized with the Holy Ghoft." Acts i. 5.

AND as to the manner of its adminiftration, he has not declared one word about its being by dipping in outward water. On the contrary, what he does exprefsly declare, as to its adminiftration by his apoftles, fhews it to be by and through the efficacy of their powerful gofpel miniftry. They were to teach, baptizing: and that not into water; but " into the name of the Father, and of the Son, and of the Holy Ghoft." And even this very author, in reciting this paffage, this great commiffion both affirms it to be " the firft account of baptifm as a Chriftian inftitution: and renders it " into the name," &c. p. 39. Now if, as he afferts, this is " the firft account of baptifm as a Chriftian inftitution," and if this is fo very different from that which was in water, that it is into the eternal name, how could he add water to this inftitution, and yet repeatedly maintain the abfolute neceffity of a plain and exprefs declaration from Chrift himfelf, both as to the nature, end and defign, and alfo the due manner of performing and receiving Chriftian
baptifm?

baptifm? This he urges again and again. See
page 45. " It cannot be doubted Jefus Chrift
fufficiently declared to his firft and immediate
followers, the whole of what he defigned fhould
be underftood by or implied in this duty; for
this being a pofitive inftitution, depending entirely upon his will, and not defigned to contain
any thing in it but what he himfelf fhould pleafe
to affix to it, it muft follow, that he declared his
mind about it fully and plainly ; becaufe, otherwife, he muft be fuppofed to inftitute a duty of
which no one could have any notion without his
inftitution, and at the fame time not to inftruct
his followers fufficiently what that duty was to
be." If this is good reafoning againft fprinkling
infants, why not as good againft dipping adults
in material water, fince Chrift never once mentions either as belonging to his baptifm? And
yet this fenfible author will not allow any thing
at all in it, or to be underftood, or even implied
in it, but what Chrift fully and plainly declared
his mind about: and then queries, " Where has
Jefus Chrift declared his mind, and declared it
fully and plainly, that infants are to receive
Chriftian baptifm ?" Now, ferious reader, let us
juft vary the terms of this queftion, and afk,
" Where has Jefus Chrift declared his mind fully
and plainly—nay, where has he declared it, at all,
that adults are to be baptized in water? or where
has he ever declared material water to pertain to
his baptifm ?" I believe the text where he has
declared this is not in the Bible, any more than
the other ; and alfo that dipping adults outwardly, is no more the baptifm Chrift ordained, than
fprinkling infants; and that the foregoing reafoning

[105]

foning is as fubftantially conclufive in one cafe, as the other.

But he goes on, and afks, " Is not our Saviour's commiffion far from declaring fully and plainly in favour of children's baptifm, perfectly filent on this head?" And I afk, is it not as perfectly filent about water? But he further afks, " does it fay any more than this, make difciples, converts, believers, amongft all nations, and baptize them?" Here I anfwer, yes; it is not only perfectly filent as to water, as not at all intended therein; it exprefsly enjoins into what they are to be baptized, the name of the Father, &c. But had it faid no more than make difciples, baptizing them, he who prefumes to add water, adds that which Chrift has no where enjoined; but has emphatically diftinguifhed from his baptifm. And he who feparates baptizing from teaching, in this commiffion, and reprefents the baptifm here enjoined, as enjoined to be otherwife adminiftered than by the baptizing miniftry of the gofpel, puts afunder what Chrift here plainly joined together.

Page 41, 42, he fays, " When therefore our bleffed Saviour, after his refurrection, inftituted his facrament of baptifm, if infants were to be received to it, it cannot be doubted that he himfelf fufficiently declared this to his firft and immediate followers, which fufficient and only authentic declaration muft appear in fome paffage of the New Teftament. " There feems" (fays he) " the greateft reafon to expect fome exprefs declaration on this head, becaufe otherwife men who had hitherto been ufed to exclude infants, and to look upon them no way concerned in the ordinance of baptifm, would be likely, ftill to.

H   pafs

pafs them by, and not think of them as coming
within the reach of their frefh commiffion. Men
who, during John's miniftry, had already baptized an infinite multitude of the adult only
amongft the Jews, would naturally conclude,
on their being fent forth to practife the fame
rite among the Gentiles, that with them alfo
the adult only were proper fubjects, unlefs there
appeared fomething upon the face of their commiffion to teach them otherwife." Now does not
this hold altogether as forcibly againft immerfion in water? let us read the argument thus :
when our Saviour, after his refurrection, commiffionated his difciples to adminifter his one
faving baptifm, if outward water belonged to it,
it cannot be doubted that he himfelf fufficiently
declared this to his firft and immediate followers;
which fufficient and only authentic declaration
muft appear in fome paffage of the New Teftament. There feems the greateft reafon to expect
fome exprefs declaration on this head; becaufe,
otherwife, men who had hitherto been ufed to
hear water baptifm called John's, and pointedly
diftinguifhed from Chrift's, and Chrift's exprefsly
declared to be quite another thing, the Holy
Ghoft and fire, in which it were very abfurd to
fuppofe material water to have any part, might
be very likely ftill to reject water, as not at all
within the meaning of a commiffion confined
wholly to the one faving baptifm and miniftry of
the gofpel, which was to continue to the end of
the world, and which could not be adminiftered
without the immediate prefence and help of Chrift
in fpirit; and therefore required their waiting at
Jerufalem, till they were " endued with power
from on high," before they could execute the
commiffion.

MEN

MEN who, during John's miniftry, had baptized many of the Jews into his watery baptifm,
and had confidered it only as his, and as preparing the way for Chrift's, might very naturally,
on being fent to baptize the Gentiles with Chrift's
baptifm, and for qualification, promifed his divine prefence or the enduement of " power from
on high," conclude that water baptifm was ftill
but John's, and required no more power from
above to adminifter it now than before; but that
Chrift's, being, as they had ever been taught,
entirely a different baptifm, required quite different qualifications to adminifter it; and which,
accordingly, they were promifed to receive, and
directed to wait for, before they went forth, or
indeed could poffibly go forth, in this commiffion. All this, the very nature of Chrift's baptifm, the manner and terms of the commiffion,
and the qualifications exprefsly pointed out therein, as neceffary to its execution, might naturally
lead them to conclude, unlefs there had alfo
fomething appeared upon the face of their commiffion to teach them otherwife, and turn their
minds from Chrift's to John's baptifm; which
yet, in itfelf, were, in fuch a commiffion, un-
accountably abfurd. But prejudice has fuch a
powerful influence, that many texts are read and
quoted in fupport of elementary water, which
fpeak only of the fpiritual water of the word. I
even admire at the mifapplication of a confiderable number, in this way, by the author now mentioned; and perhaps I may, before I have done,
point fome of them out; though I aim not at
controverfy, but the advancement of all, beyond
figns and fhadows, to the life and fubftance.
And this I think will be the cafe with fuch as

fully

fully adhere to the beſt part of the ſentiments contained in their beſt writings ; as for inſtance, the foregoing in the preſent author's account.

AND again, p. 46. " A limited commiſſion amounts to a prohibition of the things not therein contained." This he doubtleſs thought, and doubtleſs many of his readers ſtill think it concluſive againſt infant ſprinkling. I think it as much ſo againſt outward immerſion. The commiſſion is as much limited in one caſe as the other, and as much " amounts to a prohibition." Let then this ſentiment be admitted in its full force and latitude, and it will lead to the unſhadowy diſpenſation of goſpel realities, to the baptiſm that now ſaves us. But inſtead of this, too many are acting, as he ſays the Romaniſt does, about infallibility, p. 71. " Thus" (ſays he) " the Romaniſt, in an affair whoſe nature admits of none but poſitive evidence, endeavours to make up the want of it by inference, and reaſoning from fitneſs. Such an inſtitution there was under the Old Teſtament, therefore it remains under the New." And do not both Pædo and Antipædo-Baptiſts endeavour to make out water to Chriſt's baptiſm, which is wholly wanting in the words of his commiſſion, and wholly repugnant to the nature and deſign of his baptiſm, by inference ? And is it not urged upon us by them, from what was under a former diſpenſation too, and that a decreaſing one, and deſigned to terminate, and be fulfilled in Chriſt?—whoſe goſpel and baptiſm is the power of God unto ſalvation to true believers ?—p. 61, he ſpeaks of ſureties for infants, as entirely a ſupplement.—I ſay the ſame of water.—It is entirely a ſupplement,

ment, that men ftrive hard to add to the gofpel.
—But in the matter of an inftituted duty, he
maintains " no one can be a judge but the infti-
tutor himfelf of what he defigned fhould be contained in it, and becaufe, fuppofing him not to
have fpoken his mind plainly about it, it is impoffible that any other perfon (to whom the in-
ftitutor himfelf never revealed his defign) fhould
make up that defect : all that is added, therefore
(fays he) " to Chrift's inftitution as a neceffary
part of it, ought to be efteemed only as the in-
vention of thofe who add it: and the more there
is added (let it be done with never fo much fo-
lemnity, and never fo great pretences to authority)
the lefs there is remaining of the fimplicity of the
inftitution, as Chrift himfelf left it." p. 61.

WHAT pity it is, reader, that men who can
argue fo clofely againft human inferences, additions, fupplements and inventions, do not fo
feel the force of their own arguments, as to leave
all additions, and come home to the naked fimplicity of Chrift's inftitutions, as he himfelf has
left them to us.—But he goes on faying, " I am
the more folicitous to obferve this, and to imprefs it upon the minds of Chriftians, becaufe it
is the only thing that can either prevent or cure
the miftakes of many fincere Chriftians upon this
fubject*." He fays, p. 54. " the people called

* And yet, after all his folicitude to obferve and imprefs
thefe fentiments, he has himfelf, throughout his performe-
ance, miftakenly kept up, and endeavoured to maintain, the
addition and fupplement of an outward fign (for he repeatedly calls it a fign himfelf) to the inftitution of an important
and foul-faving ordinance of the gofpel. So hard is it
either to prevent or cure the miftakes of many fincere
Chriftians upon this fubject.

Quakers

Quakers are of opinion, that the baptifm of the
fpirit is the alone Chriftian baptifm, and the baptifm of water belonged only to the difpenfation
of John, But in the cafe of Cornelius we have
an inftance under the Chriftian difpenfation, and
upon the call of the Gentiles to the faith of the
gofpel, wherein it appears the Apoftle Peter is
fo far from concluding the baptifm of the fpirit,
renders that of water unneceffary, that he infers
directly the contrary, viz. no man ought to be
againft their baptifm in water, becaufe they had,
previoufly, received the baptifm of the Holy
Ghoft. Then baptifm with the Holy Ghoft was
the proof and reafon of their right to the baptifm
of water."

This argument fhould be well examined; no
doubt it weighs much with many, and feems to
them unanfwerable: but to me there is fomething
in it which tends directly to the confirmation of
the Quaker's doctrine, and the overthrow of his
own. The Quaker fays, " the baptifm of the
fpirit is the alone Chriftian baptifm, and the baptifm of water belonged only to the difpenfation
of John." But this author, throughout his " plain
account," infifts on immerfion in water, as the
baptifm of Chrift. Now there is but " one Lord,
one faith, and one baptifm," belonging to the
Chriftian difpenfation—but here this author, three
times, mentions exprefsly both the baptifm of
the Spirit, or Holy Ghoft, and the baptifm of
water, as diftinct things, as two baptifms, and
urges them being both ufed in the cafe of Cornelius, as proof that water baptifm belongs to the
gofpel.—Will he fay, Chrift inftituted two baptifms? if not, as here were two mentioned, it is

plain

plain one only of them was Chrift's. If Chrift's
is but one, and that one be that of the Holy
Ghoft, then that with water is not Chrift's, but,
as the Quaker fays, was John's. On the other
hand, if Chrift's is but one, and that one be
immerfion in elementary water, then that of the
Holy Ghoft is not Chrift's.—So that this inftance,
inftead of proving water baptifm to be Chrift's,
proves the quite contrary; and powerfully confirms the Quakers' doctrine, that it was only
John's, and was continued through condefcenfion
to the weaknefs of many, in that early ftate of
things in the Chriftian church. And as it was
adminiftered to fome before, and to others after
they received Chrift's baptifm of the Holy Ghoft,
I think nothing can be gathered from this inftance
in fupport of the right, the divine right, as he elfe-
where calls it, of outward immerfion under the
gofpel, unlefs it be granted that fuch as received
immerfion before the baptifm of the fpirit, had
no right to it; the which to grant, is at once
giving up feveral of the fuppofed ftrong holds in
favour of water.

Indeed whoever attempts to prove figns and
fhadows part of the gofpel, will ever meet with
infurmountable difficulties: hence we find many
attendant on every attempt (however ingenioufly
executed) to dignify water baptifm to the degree
of an ordinance with Jefus.—But when we once
come to the genuine fimplicity of the gofpel, thefe
difficulties vanifh; and nothing feems more natural and eafy, nothing more confonant to plain
fcripture, and the neceffity of occafions, than thefe
frequent condefcenfions, in times of weaknefs,
and therein thofe diverfe continuations of things,

H 4

in point of obligation, ceafed, which are recorded in the New Teftament.—Indeedt his very condef-cenfion is one eminent difplay both of the wif-dom and compaffionate goodnefs of our Saviour. —It exhibits him equal to all ftates and condi-tions, "touched with a feeling of our infirmities," commiferating our weaknefs, taking the lambs in his bofom, and " gently leading thofe that are with young ;" feeding them with food they could bear, milk before ftrong meat ; and indulging them with figns, till they could fee the all-fuffi-ciency of the fubftance, to which all the figns pointed—" there is a time to every purpofe ;"— and, fays Chrift, if I have told you earthly things, and ye believe not, how fhall ye believe if I tell you of heavenly things ?" John iii. 12. He knew what was in man, knew all his attachments and weakneffes, and gracioufly ftooped to the loweft, darkeft and moft literal ftate of fincere feekers; waiting patiently their gradual advance-ment to a ftate of pure fpiritual worfhip, void of " all old things," of every fign and fymbol.— And I have a full perfuafion and belief, that fuch is his condefcending goodnefs and forbearance, in our days, towards great numbers of fincere-hearted difciples, who are ftill, even in reading the New Teftament, fo far under the vail as not to perceive the abolition of certain ceremonials, which never did, and in the nature of things never could belong to the gofpel : and the travail and prayer of my foul is, that they may not, as too many certainly and forrowfully do to their great hindrance in the true Chriftian progrefs, fettle down, and ftick in thefe things ; but may pafs forward into the myftery of Chrift, till they experience the vail entirely done away in him.—

The

The vail is done away in Chriſt.—This is the
joyful experience of ſuch· as are livingly in him
the life, the ſubſtance, the Lord from heaven,
the quickening ſpirit, the light of men, and inward hope of glory: but a mere profeſſion of
Chriſt can never do away the vail.—" The covering is ſpread over the face of all nations"—and is
as thick, and dark over the minds of nominal
Chriſtians, yea, thouſands who are high in profeſſion of Chriſt, and zealous in exterior performances, as it is over any perſons whatever, or ever
was over the Jews in reading Moſes.—And though
the God of all grace is pleaſed to permit many
upright hearted men and women to remain ſo
under the vail as ſtill to uſe and plead for theſe
exteriors; yea, ſome who are in a degree preachers of the goſpel; yet, bleſſed be his holy name,
he is not without, but has raiſed up and preſerved
many living witneſſes, from time to time, to the
pure ſpirituality of his goſpel kingdom, who are
truly of the inward heart, "circumciſion, which
worſhip God in the ſpirit, and rejoice in Chriſt
Jeſus, and have no confidence in the fleſh,"
Phil. iii. 3. Theſe dare not confide in touch,
taſte, handle, or become ſubject to ordinances, in
theſe things, which periſh with the uſing. Col. ii.
20, 21, 22.

MANY ſuch there are, even in our day, who
can truly " thank God" that he has ſhewn them
clearly the emptineſs and abrogation of all theſe
things, and can truly declare, with Paul, touching
water baptiſm, that " God ſent them not to baptize, but to preach the goſpel." And it is believed, that if the preachers of our day were all
to wait till God ſent them to baptize in water, or

not

not to run without his commiſſion and ſending, we ſhould ſoon ſee a total ceſſation of the practice; and no real loſs to Chriſtianity neither.—Indeed, if they were all to wait his ſending, before and until they commence preachers, there would doubtleſs be abundantly leſs of that teaching which is not baptizing. And is it not highly probable, that one great reaſon why many, under ſuch teaching, cannot believe the goſpel miniſtry is truly according to the goſpel commiſſion, " teach, baptizing,"—in their non-experience of the power and efficacy of the pure living miniſtry of the goſpel, which is always in the power of God, and is more or leſs to the ſalvation of them that believe ? But where there is a living miniſtry in purity preſerved, and where the living word, thus livingly preached, is mixed with true faith (which is ever of the operation of God) in them that hear it ; theſe can ſet to their ſeal, that ſuch do really " miniſter to them the ſpirit." See Gal. iii. 5. " he therefore that miniſtereth to you the ſpirit." Here " the excellency of the power is of God," even though we have this treaſure in earthen veſſels, 2 Cor. iv. 7.—Though it is men, that out of this good treaſure of the heart bring forth excellent things, " miniſter the ſpirit," impart ſpiritual gifts, and actually baptize into the life and ſpirit, name and power, of the Father, &c.—yea, beget ſouls to God ; as Paul ſays, " I have begotten you through the goſpel," 1 Cor. iv. 15.; yet the inſtruments have no ſufficiency of themſelves ;—their " ſufficiency is of God," who maketh them able miniſters of the New Teſtament, " not of the letter, but of the ſpirit," 2 Cor. iii. 5, 6.—Hence Paul ſaid, he would " know not the ſpeech of them which are puffed up, up, but the power. For the kingdom of God is not in word, but in power." 1 Cor. iv. 19, 20. Were all to keep ftrictly to this life and power of the kingdom, thefe figns would ceafe for ever; and we fhould have no other miniftry, but the pure baptizing miniftry of the gofpel. And here arifeth the neceffity of waiting upon the Lord, for the renewal of ftrength, and qualification for all gofpel miniftry; that fo the power may, indeed be of God; as the apoftles waited to be " endued with power from on high."—And thofe who fo wait, and dare not run of themfelves, or preach in their own time, or at one time, becaufe they have at another, they follow the great fhepherd, learn his experience, and are led in his footfteps :—their hour is not always ;—it frequently is not yet come, as was the cafe with him : but great is their advantage, by this experience and limitation ; for when it does come, it comes with power; and they know the life and meaning of Chrift's words, John xx. 21. " as my Father hath fent me, even fo fend I you." And furely he was fent of the Father, to baptize with the Holy Ghoft, and did do it, and that even in preaching the gofpel to the meek. And as he was anointed for this fervice by the Spirit of the Lord, that was upon him, as before noticed, in order that his minifters might be qualified for the like fervice, and be fent in like manner as he was ; immediately " when he had faid this, he breathed on them, and faith unto them, receive ye the Holy Ghoft," ver. 22.; and thus qualified by the fame anointing, and fent forth in the fame fervice, they were enabled to work the fame works, according to his promife, John xiv. 12, " verily, verily" (mark the certainty

tainty of it) " I fay unto you, he that believeth on me, the works that I do, fhall he do alfo; and greater works than thefe fhall he do; becaufe I go unto my Father."—But why becaufe he went to the Father? becaufe he would then pray the Father, and the Comforter, the Spirit of Truth, fhould be fent to abide with them for ever, to lead and guide them into all truth, and qualify them to work the works of God.

Paul exhorts Timothy, " that good thing which was committed unto thee, keep by the Holy Ghoft, which dwelleth in us," 2 Tim. i. 14. And was not this good thing truly, as Paul calls it, " the gift of God?" and yet was it not in Timothy by the putting on of Paul's hands? 2 Tim. i. 6. Thus we fee, as in other inftances, " through laying on of the Apoftles hands the Holy Ghoft was given," Acts viii. 18. and why not as eafily by their preaching? It is evident, that it was given by their preaching, which was in the divine power, as well as by the laying on of hands, in the fame power, and that too in this very inftance, the cafe of Timothy; for fays Paul to him, " neglect not the gift that is in thee, which was given by prophecy, with the laying on of the hands of the Prefbytery," 1 Tim. iv. 14.

Here Paul declares this gift of God was given by prophecy, as well as by laying on hands. And what is prophecy? It is preaching the gofpel; for " he that prophecieth" (fays Paul) " fpeaketh unto men to edification, and exhortation and comfort," 1 Cor. xiv. 3. Great edification and comfort indeed attend fuch truly gofpel prophe-cying and teaching, when thereby he that thus

fpeaketh

speaketh unto men, " ministereth unto them the spirit," the gift of God, that is thus given to them, as a good thing indeed, and which, after they have received it, they cannot keep it, " but by the Holy Ghost that is in them."—It is the spirit that first quickeneth ; and as these quicken- ings are attended to, an increasing with the in- crease of God is happily experienced; even "grace, for" (the faithful improvement of) " grace." And after all improvements and communications of grace, or the Holy Ghost, it is still this alone that can enable us to keep this precious treasure, which we have thus graciously received from God; being given to us, of him, in our earthen ves- sels. It is neither speaking, nor laying on of hands, in a formal manner, that can convey di- vine influence to the soul, or qualify for divine service. The power is only of God ; and he that is not immediately impowered of God, has no- thing more to do, either with preaching or laying on hands, than Simon the sorcerer, who would have bought with money the privilege of com- municating the Holy Ghost, that he might trade with it, as I conclude, and make money by the business.

It is probable the sign of laying on of hands was, in that weak and early state of the church, or of many young converts, made use of as a con- firmation, thereby strengthening their faith in the truth of the gospel, and in the power attending the apostles; but is neither needful where the gospel is generally established, nor, out of the life, any more availing than the brazen serpent was to Israel, after its real use was ceased, and they were become ensnared by an idolatrous at-

tachment

tachment to it, and dependence on it. The minds
of men, not fingle to divine light, are ever liable
to miftake the real ufe and defign of fuch things;
to continue them out of all proper feafon, and
rely too much upon them. Hence the continuation of water baptifm, bread and wine, laying
on of hands, &c. among Chriftians, even to this
day, as of Ifrael's lifelefs looking to that mere
piece of brafs, for feveral hundred years, formerly,
and long after its real ufe was over, and when
no good was derived from their formal looking
to it.

ANANIAS was fent to Paul exprefsly, Acts ix.
17, that he might " be filled with the Holy
Ghoft." Then furely he inftrumentally difpenfed
or miniftered it to him; or (which is the fame
thing) baptized him with it.

Some contend againft baptizing fpiritually by
teaching in the power of the gofpel, and urge
that the gift of tongues always attended the baptifm of the Holy Ghoft. If fo, who have this
baptifm in our day? Will it be granted that
none are now baptized with the baptifm of Chrift?
Then the faints now receive none but John's.
But there are divers inftances in the New Teftament of perfons baptized with the Holy Ghoft,
where not a word is faid of their fpeaking with
tongues, as the attentive reader may fee for himfelf.

PETER, in relating his vifit to Cornelius, mentions the angel's faying to him, to wit, that he
(Peter) fhould tell him words whereby he and
his houfe fhould be faved. This fhews his words
would

would be with baptizing efficacy; that he would, as he certainly did, baptize them with the Holy Ghost: he taught baptizingly, according to commiffion; and he himfelf evidently confiders that baptifm with the Holy Ghost, which they received through his teaching, as an exact accomplifhment both of this faying of the angel, and of our Lord's promife in regard to the baptifm of the Holy Ghost. Do, kind reader, examine the paffage for thyfelf, Acts xi. where the angel, fpeaking of Peter, fays to Cornelius, verfe 14, "who fhall tell thee words, whereby thou and all thy houfe fhall be faved." In the very next fentence, to fhew how exactly this was verified, Peter fays, verfe 15. "and as I began to fpeak, the Holy Ghost fell on them, as on us at the beginning." Here he plainly connects their reception of the Holy Ghost, through his miniftry, with the faying of the angel, that he fhould tell them words, by which they fhould be faved. Indeed, how could he poffibly tell them words by which they fhould be faved, unlefs baptizing influence attended his words? Nothing ever faves the foul, without the baptifm of the Holy Ghost. Had I heard the angel tell Cornelius, that Peter would tell him words by which he fhould be faved, I think it would to me have been fufficient evidence that Peter's words fhould be with baptizing power. And this I think might be depended on; feeing nothing faves fhort of "the wafhing of regeneration, and renewing of the Holy Ghost." And on this ground we might take it for certain, from this faying of the angel, that Peter's powerful teaching was to prove baptizing to Cornelius and his houfhold, whether Chrift had ever verbally commiffionated him and

the

the other apoftles to teach baptizingly or not; and
whether Peter had ever related that he did fo or
not. But feeing Chrift did fo commiffionate
them, and feeing the angel did declare, that Peter
fhould deliver words by which men fhould be
faved; and feeing none can be faved without the
one only faving and fpiritual baptifm; and feeing
they received this, as Peter began to fpeak, the
Holy Ghoft then falling on them; and feeing
Peter himfelf evidently confidered its fo falling
on them as the baptifm of the Holy Ghoft; and
immediately, in the very next words, applied
our Lord's promife to what then took place,
through his miniftry, faying, verfe 16. " then
remembered I the word of the Lord, how that he
faid, John indeed baptized with water; but ye
fhall be baptized with the Holy Ghoft:" I think
all thefe facts and confiderations, taken together,
amount to a very full and ftrong confirmation,
that the miniftry of the gofpel is a baptizing
miniftry, and that men did inftrumentally baptize
with the Holy Ghoft. And this will affuredly be
the cafe, as long as Chrift continues to be with
his minifters, and they thereby continue to preach
the gofpel, as it was preached in the primitive
times, " with the Holy Ghoft fent down from
heaven." And this (it is the unfhaken faith of
fome) will be the cafe " even unto the end of the
world. Amen."

THIS account of Peter's, refpecting the baptifm of Cornelius and his family with the Holy
Ghoft, through his miniftry, is fo connected and
expreffed by him, as to confirm his meaning,
where, afterwards, he fpeaks of the baptifm which
now faves us, to be, that this faving baptifm is
the

the fame by which Cornelius and his houfe were baptized, while he was delivering thofe words, by which the angel had faid they fhould be faved. Peter knew no figure could fave, any more than the " blood of bulls and of goats" could " take away fins;" and therefore, in telling what is the baptifm which faves (which is feveral times already remarked) he alfo carefully fhews us what it is not, left his mention of the word water fhould draw fuch as were too outward in their views to truft in or continue the ufe of that which only puts away the outward filth of the flefh, or of the body. And his commanding Cornelius and his houfe to be baptized, no more proves he had a commiffion to baptize with water, than Paul's baptizing Crifpus and Gaius proves he had a commiffion for it, which he declares he had not ; nor yet a whit more than his circumcifing Timothy, and purifying in the temple, and James' directing the fick to be anointed with oil in the name of the Lord, proves a divine commiffion for all thefe things. Had Paul given a circumftantial relation of his baptizing the few he did baptize in water, without mentioning that he was not fent to do it, or thanking God that he did it in fo few inftances, it had been as ftrong in favour of the practice, as any inftances of its adminiftration by the reft of the apoftles. This he might have done, as well as others, though he was not fent to adminifter that baptifm. And do not all fee it would in reality have been no true fupport of the practice ? Yet how eagerly would it have been claimed, as a fupport thereof, juft as are the inftances where others ufed it.

I   Now

Now let us fuppofe they had all teftified (and I can fee no reafon why they might not, as truly as Paul) that Chrift fent them not fo to baptize; that they did it in condefcenfion, and thanked God that they did it no more; what then would become of all thofe inftances, now fo confidently urged as proof that a mere figurative immerfion is the faving baptifm of Jefus? They did divers things without commiffion, and yet do not exprefsly declare they were not fent to do them. Does their omiffion of fuch a declaration infer they had a commiffion? By no means. Neither does their not declaring they were not fent to adminifter elementary baptifm, infer they had a commiffion for that. But, fay many, Chrift gave them a commiffion to baptize. Very true: and the minds of men looking outward for the meaning and accomplifhment of many things that are inward and fpiritual, has induced them miftakenly, among other inftances, to underftand a commiffion exprefsly to baptize into the eternal name, as meaning into water; and thus to retain, as a gofpel ordinance, a mere figurative, preparatory, decreafing and terminating inftitution. Some think it muft have been by divine commiffion that the apoftles baptized in water, becaufe it was in the name of the Lord. But we fee the anointing of the fick with oil, was alfo in the name of the Lord. And yet I know of none who now hold to a divine commiffion for this practice. But we may take notice, that neither this, nor water baptifm, " was into the name of the Father, and of the Son, and of the Holy Ghoft." No, there is not one inftance of this form of words in all the Bible, in the ufe of water, which furely we may

conclude

conclude would have been the case, had the commiffion defigned an outward dipping; for, in
that cafe, that muft have been the ordained form
of words; but as water was not meant, the commiffion contains no form of words at all to be
ufed in baptifm; but the words into the name, &c.
exprefs the very nature, power, and divine efficacy of the baptifm they were to adminifter. It
was not their own, it was not John's, it was not
water, it was not any thing that they could adminifter at any other time, than when fpecially
" endued with power from on high;" and therefore this they were to wait for, and were promifed to receive, as their qualification, from
him who has all power.

Now he who had all power, was " Lord even
of the Sabbath day," Mat. xii. 8. and juft as
much Lord of every other fign, and has equally
fulfilled them all, and redeemed his people from
every yoke of mere ceremonial obfervations;—
for he was made of a woman, " made under the
law, to redeem thofe that were under the law,"
Gal. iv. 4.—And if Chrift was made under the
law, furely John was alfo under it, as I have before advanced; nor was it ever totally abolifhed,
even as a law of carnal or outward ordinances,
till Chrift rofe from the dead.—And this holds
good inwardly with the true Chriftian traveller in
his own experience—" he that hath an ear, let
him hear."

But as John was under the law (though advanced near to the kingdom) Chrift has, in re-
deeming his people from all ceremonials of the
law, alfo redeemed them from water baptifm,

which

which indeed was frequently in fome fort practifed
under the law, long before John ; as appears by
the very precepts of the law—and which is allowed by the author of the " plain account" before mentioned ; for fpeaking of baptifm in the
days of the apoftles, he fays, " the principal
fcene of baptifm lay in a country where immerfion was quite familiar, and muft, by the very
laws of their religion, come into daily ufe through
all parts of the land," p. 29. Baptifm in water
being therefore a ceremonial of the law, was,
though differently ufed by John, completely
ended, with every other ceremony thereof, when
Jefus rofe triumphant from the grave, led captivity captive, and gave fpiritual gifts unto men.
And when he rifes fo in us, and completely puts
all things under him, in our fouls, we fhall all find
there are no figns or fymbols in the gofpel, as
ftanding ordinances thereof.—John's ufing water
baptifm a little differently from what had been
ufual before, made no difference as to its perpe-
tuity, though that difference might have taught
the Jews, had their ears been open enough
to have heard it aright, that he who was
coming after him would make great alterations,
and remove thofe things that could be fhaken,
that thofe only which could not be fhaken might
remain.—There is abundant evidence in fcripture,
that Chrift never intended to incorporate any of
the old rituals into his pure religion and worfhip.
—Thus he taught the woman of Samaria, at the
well, that the true worfhip was inward, " in
fpirit and in truth,"—and turned her mind from
outward water to the inward, John iv. And when
John's difciples came to him, faying, " why do
we and the pharifees faft oft, but thy difciples faft
                                        not ?"

not?" Mat. ix. 14. he firſt ſhows the time of
mourning is not while the bridegroom's comfort-
ing preſence is enjoyed; but that, when he was
taken from them, then they would faſt: which
ſhows the faſt he meant was inward.—And, in
the next place, to ſhow the impropriety of uniting the ceremonials of the law, as outward faſts,
waſhings, &c. with the goſpel, the life, the
ſubſtance—he tells them, "no man putteth a
piece of new cloth into an old garment," &c.
"neither do men put new wine into old bottles,"
&c. plainly inculcating, that his goſpel was the
new and living way—his new cloth, the robe of
pure righteouſneſs—the garment of ſalvation; his
new wine, the wine he drinks new with his choſen,
in his Father's inward and ſpiritual kingdom—
and therefore is put only into the new bottles, the
hearts of the ſanctified; that ſo their hearts might
be animated, and rejoice in his ſalvation, out of
all formality and ritual obſervances; for that he
was not come, with his new wine, to ſupply the
old bottles of law ceremonies, or animate therewith the vaniſhing diſpenſation of types and
ſhadows,—nor with his new cloth, to patch up
the old garment of thoſe "carnal ordinances,"
impoſed on them until the time of reformation,
Heb. ix. 10. which was only "a figure for the
time then preſent," v. 9. Nay, verily, this was
not his intention;—not the deſign of the Father
in ſending him—he came to aboliſh all theſe, and
ſo to bring in everlaſting righteouſneſs; and
which, wherever it is completely brought in, entirely ſupercedes the neceſſity of all theſe outward
ordinances, and aboliſhes them forever.

I 3

IT is further obfervable, that Chrift's directions about fafting, point plainly to that which is
inward, and wherein thofe who faft according to
them " appear not unto men to faft," Mat. vi.
18. Indeed, it being his peculiar office to fulfil
and abolifh the ceremonial obfervances, I believe
we fhall find, by a careful and illuminated perufal
of all his parables and difcourfes, that he never
on any occafion expreffed any thing for the perpetuation of outward figns, but, on the contrary,
very repeatedly, and on almoft every occafion
that furnifhed proper opportunity, pointed out,
though often times very obfcurely, at leaft to this
world's wifdom, the unceremonious and purely
fpiritual nature of his kingdom.—But thefe are
things which " the vulture's eye" (though very
prying) " hath not feen," Job xxviii. 7. They
are only " fpiritually difcerned." The natural
man (with all his talk of Chrift and gofpel ordinances) cannot know them. See i Cor. ii. 14.

CHAP.

C H A P. VI.

All baptized with Chriſt's baptiſm are members of his church, and none elſe. Six queries; which, rightly anſwered, will determine which is Chriſt's baptiſm. Divers other queries. Paul's care to avoid running in vain; hence he omits open proclamation againſt circumciſion, at Jeruſalem, though he had preached againſt it among Gentiles. Not ſtrange, then, John's baptiſm was ſtill in vogue. The TWELVE *baptized only by John, in water. They could adminiſter John's, without the power they were to wait for to adminiſter Chriſt's. Putting on Chriſt in baptiſm, is putting on the armour of light. The word for* teach *in the commiſſion, not the common word* didaſko, *but* matheteuo, *to diſciple,* inſtruct *into the kingdom of heaven. Sprinklers and dippers both greatly err about Iſrael's baptiſm in the cloud and ſea. It ſupports neither. " Plain account" correĉted in this reſpeĉt. The author of it allows the diſciples the uſe of water baptiſm, during Chriſt's miniſtry on earth, was the ſame as John's. It is the ſoul needs purgation. Water cannot do it. Diverſe texts ſhewing plainly the name is often uſed for the life, preſence, power of the Lord.*

THERE is a baptiſm by which every member is initiated into the body of Chriſt. As ſure as any are thus baptized, they are mem-

bers

bers of Chriſt.—If any are not thus baptized, they are not of Chriſt's church.

Now, Query 1. What is the baptiſm, without which none can be members of Chriſt's church—and which none can be baptized with, but they immediately become members?

Query 2. Are all ſure to be members of Chriſt's true church, who are baptized in water?

Query 3. Has Chriſt two baptiſms? See Eph. iv. 5. " one Lord, one faith, and one baptiſm." No more two goſpel baptiſms than two Lords, and two faiths.

Query 4. Does not Paul plainly ſay, " by one ſpirit we are all baptized into one body—and have been all made to drink into one ſpirit?" 1 Cor. xii. 13.

Query 5. Can any other but this, which baptizeth into the one body of Chriſt, be the one initiatory and ſaving baptiſm of Chriſt?

Query 6. Can that be the one baptiſm of Chriſt, which thouſands may be baptized with, and yet not become members of his true church, but remain in the gall of bitterneſs, and bond of iniquity? o

I think theſe ſix queries, rightly anſwered, will determine which is the one initiatory and ſaving baptiſm of Chriſt in the goſpel. Is it not ſtrange that men do not ſee it?—Why do they ſtick in the practices of the Apoſtles ſo rigidly,

in

in regard to John's baptifm and the fupper, and fo eafily get over divers other of their practices? —Would it not have been a ftrange and almoft unheard of thing, had thofe famous inftitutions dropt into difufe all of a fudden ?—Could it pof- fibly have been borne ?—Do we not always find it much eafier to bring people by degrees to re- ject old venerated laws and cuftoms, and adopt new ones, than to rufh on and enforce them all at once ?—Is not God a God of condefcenfion and tendernefs ? Did he not anciently lead his people Ifrael, after he brought them out of Egypt, pur- pofely a different way from the neareft, left they fhould meet with difcouragements, and return back to Egypt? Exod. xiii. 17. Would he not at leaft allow his Apoftles to exercife condefcen- fion, and go in and out before the primitive be- lievers, as they could bear it ?—Was not this evidently the cafe on divers other occafions ?— Did not Paul, in communicating to the brethren at Jerufalem how it was that he preached the gofpel among the Gentiles, to wit, void of cere- monies, and without circumcifion, do it privately, to fuch only as were grown in the truth, and able to fee the propriety of it, and to underftand that the gofpel has no fuch outward obfervations ? Gal. ii. 2.—Does he not fay, that this his care to avoid a general communication to all was, "left he fhould run, or had run in vain ?" Might it not have been wholly in vain for Paul to attempt benefiting the believers that were of the circum- cifion at Jerufalem, if he had bluntly at firft de- clared off hand, that circumcifion was abolifhed ? And was not this about the year of our Lord fifty- two, and about the feventeenth year of Paul's apoftlefhip?

It

Is it ftrange, then, that he had to circumcife
Timothy, purify in the temple, &c. on account
of the wrong zeal and attachments of the Jews,
feeing fo late in the day circumcifion fo far main-
tained its ground, that he had probably run in
vain, if he had not avoided an open declaration
of its being no gofpel ordinance ?—And is it any
ftranger, that John's baptifm fhould be in too
high eftimation to be eafily laid afide at once ?
Is water baptifm once called Chrift's in all the
Bible? Is it once called a gofpel ordinance ? Did
Chrift ever practife it ? Was John's baptifm
Chrift's ? If not, were Chrift's twelve difciples
ever baptized with Chrift's baptifm, or not? If
Chrift's is water, and yet not the fame of John's,
who baptized thefe Apoftles, feeing Jefus baptized none in water ? And we never read of the
Apoftles being baptized therein by any but John.
I have often mentioned, that the defign of water
baptifm was, that Chrift and his baptifm might
be made manifeft to Ifrael : and as this was fully
done to the Apoftles, as to his outward coming,
they needed no more water baptifm; and it feems
pretty evident they had no more than was adminiftered to them by John.—But if the commiffion,
Mat. xxviii. 19. was water, and different from
John's, why were they not baptized with it themfelves, before they went forth to baptize others ?
Is it not plain, that that commiffion, as then verbally delivered, did not qualify them with power
to adminifter the baptifm mentioned in it? Were
they not to wait for " power from on high ?" Were
they ever able to adminifter that baptifm, till they
were firft baptized with the Holy Ghoft themfelves?—Is not this a confirmation that, as they
had firft received and then oft adminiftered John's

baptifm

baptifm before, without this more powerful enduement and qualification, but could not adminifter Chrift's without it, that Chrift's was quite a
different thing from John's, and out of their reach
or ability to communicate, but as it was poured
upon them from on high, and flowed through
them upon others? " Behold how good and how
pleafant it is for brethren to dwell together in
unity; it is like the precious ointment upon the
head, that ran down upon the beard, even
Aaron's beard, that went down to the fkirts of
his garments: as the dew of Hermon, and as the
dew that defcended upon the mountains of Zion;
for there the Lord commanded the bleffing, even
life for evermore," Pfalm cxxxiii. Is there nothing in the defcending of this precious ointment,
even down to the very fkirts of the garment, in
likenefs of the living unity of the brethren, like
the dew on Mount Hermon, and like the Lord's
bleffing on Mount Zion, that may give us fome
idea of the communication of the Holy Ghoft,
through the baptized Apoftles, to and upon the
fouls of the people?—And is not this the one
plain reafon why they could not adminifter
Chrift's baptifm till livingly baptized themfelves,
as the oil could not defcend to the fkirts till it was
poured upon the head of Aaron?—And let it be
once for all ferioufly confidered—ought we not
to hold it as a certainty that if the baptifm in the
commiffion had been water, the Apoftles would
have been firft baptized with it themfelves? Or
can we fuppofe their having been baptized with
John's baptifm, by John, before they became
Chrift's difciples, fufficient to authorize them to
adminifter Chrift's? But even though this were
granted, will any fay the Apoftles never received
Chriftian baptifm themfelves? If Chrift's is water,
and

and yet not John's, how could it poffibly be difpenfed with, in the cafe of the Apoftles—in the
cafe of Apollos, and the many which Paul taught,
and begat unto God, but did not baptize in
water?—We read of none fent exprefsly to baptize in water, but John. If then, Chrift's baptifm had been with water, and yet not the fame
with John's, ought not Chrift himfelf to have
baptized his difciples with it, before he fent them
to baptize others, feeing we have no account of
any other but himfelf, that had any authority to
adminifter his baptifm, till fift baptized with it by
him?—Who among the fons of men had a right to
adminifter his baptifm, before they were baptized
with it themfelves? If none had a right fo to do,
then if his was with water, and yet different from
John's, is it not certain that his Apoftles never
received it, feeing " Jefus himfelf baptized not"
with water, and none elfe had any right to adminifter his baptifm, till themfelves were baptized
with it?—Does it not, therefore, plainly appear,
that there is no other baptifm with outward water
but John's? And did not Jefus himfelf wholly
avoid baptizing any in water, on purpofe that
it might plainly appear that there is another? Or
if there is any other with water but John's, when,
where, and by whom did it begin?—Who firft
dared to adminifter it? Would it now be thought
lawful among the Baptifts for any to adminifter
the baptifm of water, who had not received it?
And would it not have been very arrogating for
any one in that day to have intruded himfelf into
the office of an adminiftrator of Chrift's baptifm,
who had never himfelf received it? Or, had any
fo done, how would that convey a right to thofe
by fuch an one baptized, to baptize others? I
think we have all the reafon we have a right to
defire

defire to conclude, if Chrift had ordained water
baptifm, he would have adminiftered it to thofe
he had fent to adminifter it to others. And I reft
firmly perfuaded he never did ordain it, but that
all the water baptifm now practifed among Chriftians is derived from John, or elfe is altogether
unauthorized in the New Teftament. And why
do thofe who now ufe it, ufe a form of words
never once ufed by any of the Apoftles? If they
fay Chrift commanded it, then why did not his
Apoftles obey his command? Is not this another
ftrong evidence that they were not commanded
any form of words at all, nor any ufe of water,
but that the words, into the name, &c. as plainly
fhew into what they were to baptize, as water
would have been plainly fhown, had the commiffion been exprefsly to baptize into water?

It is urged by fome, that putting on Chrift,
which all do who are baptized into him, Gal. iii.
27, is giving up their names to Chrift in water
baptifm: but of thofe baptized into Chrift, in
the Apoftle's fenfe, he here declares, " ye are all
one in Chrift Jefus. And if ye be Chrift's, then
are ye Abraham's feed, and heirs according to
the promife," 28, 29. that is, real heirs of God,
and joint heirs with Chrift. This certainly is not
true of as many as are baptized into water, though
it certainly is true of as many as are baptized into Chrift. Putting on Chrift is therefore plainly
thus, " put ye on the Lord Jefus Chrift, and
make not provifion for the flefh, to fulfil the lufts
thereof," Rom. xiii. 14. that is, " caft off the
works of darknefs, and let us put on the armour
of light," v. 12. This is directly baptifm into the
name, for " God is light," and Chrift is light;
and

and putting on the whole armour of light, is truly putting on Chrift in baptifm. And it is very ftrikingly obfervable, that divers texts fpeak ex- prefsly of baptifm into Chrift; thus preferving the very intent and tenor of the commiffion; for as all the fulnefs of the Godhead dwelleth in him, and as thefe texts exprefs baptifm pofitively as being into him, and verbally in his name, as was the cafe conftantly when water was ufed, it is as evi- dent as any thing can well be, that this baptifm into him is really putting on him, the life, the fubftance, the whole armour of light—and that this anfwers the commiffion exactiy, being into the name, the life, the power, the eternal virtue itfelf; and not into water, or any thing elfe, merely and verbally in the name.—I think this meaning of the words, into the name, &c. is much confirmed by a paffage in the forementioned " plain account." The author pleads wholly for immerfion of adults in water; and to maintain it againft fprinkling of infants he fays, p. 43, 44. " the word in Matthew, rendered teach, is not the word commonly rendered teach in the New Teftament. The word commonly ufed is DI- DASKO, which occurs very often; but the other word, MATHETEUO, teach, in the baptifmal com- miffion of Matthew, is ufed only three times more in all the New Teftament, Mat. xiii. 52, every fcribe WHICH IS INSTRUCTED into the king- dom of heaven. Mat. xxvii. 57, Jofeph, who alfo himfelf was JESUS' DISCIPLE. Acts xiv, 21. when they had preached the gofpel to that city, and HAD TAUGHT many. They did not (fays he) barely preach the gofpel, but taught fo effectually, as to prevail on many to become difciples or believers. This is the plain import of the original."

DOES

Does not this make ftrongly in favour of the Quakers' doctrine ? Does it not fhew the teaching, mentioned in this great commiffion, was to be with divine power, and to prevail effectually to difciplefhip ?—Was not this the reafon they were commanded to wait to be endued with power from on high, becaufe they were now far otherwife to baptize people than they had done before ? They were now to difciple them ; that is, teach them fo livingly and effectually, as truly to baptize them into the name &c. Why elfe was this word MA-THETEUO ufed here, to exprefs this peculiar kind of powerful, difcipling, or baptifmal teaching ? a word ufed but three times more, as this author himfelf fays, in all the New Teftament.—He further fays in the fame page, that this word " implies teaching full as much as the more common word, DIDASKO. The difference is, that the former has a more precife and determinate meaning, conveying to the Apoftles this idea, viz. "fo teach the people as to perfuade them to become my difciples."

Now, ferious reader, feeing this paffage does mean teaching, but at the fame time is fo very precife and determinate in its meaning, as to convey a clear idea of great difference from the fimple common meaning of the word teach, plainly fignifying to make difciples by teaching, that is, to teach or difciple all nations, baptizing them ; let us fee how the three other paffages, where it is ufed, will concur with the doctrine of baptifm into the name, &c. The firft is Mat. xiii. 52, " every fcribe which is inftructed into the kingdom of heaven."—This is the fame word that is rendered teach in the commiffion : and here the fcribe is inftructed, taught or difcipled

into

into the kingdom of heaven.—I think this is the very baptifm enjoined in that commiſſion : it is into the very life and ſubſtance intended by the name, to wit, the life, ſtrength and virtue of the kingdom; the ſtrong tower of ſafety, which the name of the Lord ever is to the righteous, the well inſtructed or truly diſcipled ſcribe. And we ſee this ſcribe is initiated into the kingdom by teaching, and that the very teaching, diſcipling, or inſtructing, which is enjoined in the commiſſion, and which therefore required power from on high to perform, becauſe it was a very different and much more effectual teaching (as this author maintains) than that expreſſed by the common word DIDASKO, teach. The ſecond paſſage is Mat. xxvii. 57, " Joſeph, who alſo himſelf was Jeſus' diſciple." It ſeems plainly this ; he had been taught, inſtructed, diſcipled, in this more powerful way of teaching than that meant by the other word didaſko ; that is, he was a ſcribe well inſtructed into the kingdom of heaven—or baptized into the eternal holy name, which is the ſame thing ; for none can be a diſciple of Chriſt without his ſaving baptiſm.

THE third paſſage is Acts xiv. 21, " when they had preached the goſpel to that city, and had taught many"—that is, according to this author's own words, " taught ſo effectually as to prevail on many to become diſciples." " This (he adds) " is the plain import of the original." Then, it ſeems, they taught them juſt according to the commiſſion; and by which teaching they muſt have been baptized into the name ; or (which is the ſame thing) inſtructed or diſcipled into the kingdom.—But this ſenſible author adds further,
" the

" the common appellation of Chriftian believers occurring in very numerous paffages of the New Teftament, is MATHETAI, difciples. "As this" (fays he) " is the ufual name of believers in Chrift, we have the verb of it in our Lord's commiffion, where he bids his followers to go and make converts to him throughout the world;" and p. 45 he quotes " Whitby's note on Mat. xxviii. 19" that is on the very commiffion itfelf —faying, I defire any one to tell me how the apoftles could *matheteuin*, make a difciple of an heathen, or unbelieving Jew, without being *mathetai*, or teachers of them."—By all which it is clear, that both the learned Whitby, and this learned author, were fenfible that this extraordinary kind of teaching was making difciples of Chrift, believers in and real living converts to him : and it is certain none are fuch without baptifm into him—his difciples, all true believers, all his fincere converts, throughout the world, are baptized by the one fpirit into one body; they drink all into one fpirit, and are thus initiated, as well inftructed fcribes, into the kingdom of heaven.—Is it not marvellous that this writer was not, by the time he had feen and written thus much, fo far inftructed into it himfelf, as to have feen with equal clearnefs, that no part of all this had any thing to do with elementary water ?—He maintains that the word *baptizo* always means immerfion or bathing all over in water; and rejects the fprinklers, notions refpecting 1 Cor. x. 2, " and were all baptized unto Mofes in the cloud, and in the fea." The fprinklers, idea on this paffage he reprefents thus, p 28, " the cloud which hung over the children of Ifrael is a watery fubftance, fprinkling its water

K   in

in drops. The sea, which was as a wall unto them on the right hand and on the left, by force of the strong wind which blew, sent forth a great spray or sprinkling. So they were plentifully sprinkled by the cloud above, and by the waters on each side." This he cannot agree to. Let us see how he understands it, and whether he mends the matter. He thinks " a man of plain sense, not thinking of this cloud or pillar of fire, dropping down water, but of opinion—that the baptism of scripture is immersion, would be apt to carry his thoughts no further than to apprehend here, is an allusion to the custom of immersion ; the Israelites being, as it were, covered with the cloud over, and the waters on each side of them." Thus they stumble on every hand, who are vainly contending for the figures. His remark is very just, that a man of plain sense would not think of drops of water from a pillar of fire : and methinks it requires a little more than plain sense to understand immersion all over in water from this passage ; but though a man " of opinion that the baptism of scripture is immersion," might be very likely to stop short of the substance, and apprehend nothing further than an " allusion to the custom of immersion ;" yet I do not see why a man of real plain sense may not query how a pillar of fire can represent immersion in water ? Or how going through the sea on dry land, as a firm foundation, points out bathing all over in that fluctuating unstable element ? The apostle in this passage expressly declares, they eat the same spiritual meat, and that they drink of that spiritual rock that followed them, and that rock was Christ. Hence it appears, they ate and drank the very substance which the saints in all ages,
live

live by. This indeed they muſt have eaten, or elſe have had no divine life in them. Eating the outward emblems of it never gave life divine to the ſoul, any more than outward baptiſm. Their eating outward manna, and drinking outward water from the rock, could never make their ſouls alive to God, and was but typical of that "ſpiritual meat" which they alſo and as truly ate, as they did the outward: and of "that ſpiritual rock whereof they drank; for that rock was Chriſt." And why may not plain ſenſe look a little further than to an "alluſion to the cuſtom of immerſion" for the ſubſtance of their baptiſm, as well as for the ſubſtance of their eating and drinking? For ſeeing they did truly feed in greater or leſs degree on Chriſt in ſpirit, as well as on outward manna, &c. and ſo enjoyed ſomething of the very life and ſubſtance of the Lord's ſupper; why may we not believe they were in degree ſubſtantially baptized into the fellowſhip of his ſufferings, and con- formity to his death, as well as into thoſe deep outward trials and afflictions, ſo preſſingly ex- perienced by them, whilſt conducted by the pillar of fire, and whilſt purſued by their enemies at and into the midſt of the red ſea? And thus the word *baptizo* may anſwer as well to plunging into fiery trials, as into water.

Our Saviour ſays, "I have a baptiſm to be baptized with, and how am I ſtraitened till it be accompliſhed," Luke xii. 50. And can it be doubted that thoſe who really fed on Chriſt in ſpirit, in that day, were in degree truly baptized with him into ſufferings, and in ſome degree at leaſt buried with him into death? In this way I think we may ſee ſomething further in their bap- tiſm than outward immerſion, and thus reſcue

the

the pillar of fire from either dropping down
water, or importing immersion into it; and indeed there seems little or no sense in the passage
understood as speaking of either: for suppose we
understand with the plain account " an allusion
to the custom of immersion," it then amounts to
this—immersion in water is a figure of purification—and Israel's passage through the sea is a
figure of that figure; or that the apostle, in his
assertion here, that they were baptized, only had
an allusion to that figure. Now if it was nothing
but a figure of a figure, I see not how he could
positively in truth say, they were baptized.—
Either they were, or were not—if they were
properly baptized, it was inward or outward; if
it was outward, and a proper water baptism, then
either dipping, sprinkling, or any thing that
has a little resemblance and will bear an " allusion to the custom of immersion," may, for
aught I can perceive, be called baptism. Why
then contend so long and loud about the precise
mode of it? If Paul meant as he said, that they
were baptized, I think he must mean spiritually:
but if any will have it mean outward water baptism, do they not at once introduce a third kind,
or a third mode of it, different from either immersion or sprinkling? At any rate, and turn it
every way, will not the result be, either that
Paul did not mean as he said, that they really were
baptized, but only that their passage resembled
baptism, and may bear an allusion to it, or that
he meant an outward baptism, without either
dipping or sprinkling, or that he meant an inward and spiritual baptism? The two first mean-
ings I should suppose most if not all would, on
due consideration, reject—the last I am confirmed

is,

is, as before evinced, the genuine meaning of
the apoftle. He is here prefling it upon the
once livingly baptized among the Corinthians, to
hold out to the end. A few verfes before (fee
the preceding chapter, 1 Cor. ix. 24) he fays,
" fo run that ye may obtain." 25th, " every man
that ftriveth for the maftery is temperate in all
things. Now they do it' to obtain a corruptible
crown, but we an incorruptible. 26th, I therefore
fo run, not as uncertainly; fo fight I, not as one
that beateth the air; 27, but I keep under my
body, and bring it into fubjection, left that by
any means, when I have preached to others, I
myfelf fhould be a caft-away." Here he urges
his own fubjection, and the temperance of others,
as examples; and then, to enforce the caution,
imprefs the danger of their falling fhort, and if
poffible prevent their becoming caft-aways, he
pertinently reminds them how it fared with fome
of the ancient fathers who came out of Egypt with
Mofes; and who, though they had partaken of
the true fpiritual baptifm, meat and drink of the
faints, yet afterwards (fuch is the weaknefs and
danger of man) they lufted after evil things—
murmured—tempted God—committed idolatry
and fornication—and fo were overthrown in the
wildernefs.—And in full confirmation that his
aim in all this was to warn the Corinthians, he
declares, " thefe things were our examples, to
the intent that we fhould not luft after evil things,
as they alfo lufted," nor tempt Chrift, nor mur-
mur, &c. as they did; and ftrikingly adds,
" wherefore let him that thinketh he ftandeth,
take heed left he fall," v. 12. Perhaps all will
agree, that thofe thus warned by Paul had received Chriftian baptifm, whether it be agreed

or

or not what that was; and if Chriftians were in all that great danger of falling, after the example of unbelief and apoftacy here exhibited by him, and if this example was pertinent to their ftate and danger, does not that pertinency confift much in the Ifraelites having known a good degree of that which is faving, and turning from it? Nehemiah teftifies, that the Lord faw their affliction in Egypt, and heard their cry by the red fea, and gave alfo his good Spirit to inftruct them, Neh. ix. 9, 20. God was fo near and attentive to them, that he not only led them by; he even went himfelf before them in the pillar of cloud and of fire.

LET none therefore marvel that Paul fays they were baptized in the cloud, feeing that holy prefence was actually there, into which all the fpiritual Ifrael are baptized.—Mofes tells them, Deut. v. 4, " the Lord talked with you face to face" —and Ifaiah calls them the ranfomed, teftifying, li. 10, that the Lord " made the depth of the fea a way for the ranfomed to pafs over."—But in regard to their paffage through the fea, it is evident the cloud was not then over them, but behind them.—It had gone before them; but juft before their going through, we read, " the angel of God, which went before the camp of Ifrael, removed and went behind them; and the pillar of the cloud went from before their face, and ftood behind them," Exod. xiv. 19, So that unlefs immerfion all over into and under water, or at leaft an illufion to it, can be gathered from their going through the fea as on dry ground,. with a cloudy and fiery pillar behind them, I cannot fee any thing more in it for immerfion, than

for

for fprinkling; and in fact it appears to have nothing to do with either.

THIS author fays, p. 41, "the difciples of Chrift, during his miniftry on earth, as well as the difciples of John, were very well acquainted with the inftitution of baptifm;" and agrees with Whitby, that "they only baptized, as John had done, into the faith of the Meffiah which was to come, and with that baptifm of repentance, which prepared the Jews for the reception of his kingdom." By this it is conceded, that during Chrift's miniftry on earth, that baptifm which his difciples ufed was the fame as John's. No wonder then Chrift never ufed it himfelf; and as he never once ufed it either before or after his refurrection, as we do not find his twelve apoftles were ever baptized in water, but only into John's baptifm, as before noticed, it feems clear to me, that Chrift's commiffion does not contain water baptifm.— His injunction to teach the people all things that he had commanded them, includes no fuch obfervation; for he had not commanded it; nor does it appear that the difciples ever ufed it, after Chrift gave them this commiffion, in any wife as a different ordinance from what it had been before. If it was John's, and ufed by them as his before, it was afterwards but a continuation of the fame ordinance. It no where in all the Bible appears to be an ordinance of Chrift; but having been in great veneration, was indulgently continued through weaknefs, even after the refurrection.

NOTHING can be gofpel baptifm, that is not faving: it is the foul that needs purgation; the

K 4   baptifm

baptifm which effects this, cannot be that which is merely with elementary water; but muft be that which burns up the filth, and removes the defilement; that is, the baptifm into the name, the life, the cleanfing virtue of the divine nature. —Chrift's baptifm is ever defcribed as faving, and none were ever faved without it. We all know that baptifm into water, may be received by fuch as are not in any degree faved; and I think, if we exercife but the common reafon of mankind, we muft fee, that if water baptifm were faving, it were a conftant miracle, and that as oft repeated as it proved faving, even as truly a miracle as the turning water into wine; for there is nothing in a bare wafhing in outward water, that has any more effect towards an inward cleanfing, than there is in anointing with oil, or fhaving off the hair. If therefore it were the baptifm of Chrift, it muft either be a ftanding miraculous purification of fouls by outward application, or a thing not faving; but the baptifm of Chrift is that which now faves us, and is in its own nature and operation, as truly and conftantly faving to the foul, as wafhing in water is cleanfing to the body. In proportion to the degree in which the body is wafhed in water, it is cleanfed by the outward putting away the filth of the flefh; and in proportion to the degree in which any foul experienceth the baptifm of Chrift, it infallibly produceth inward fanctification, by putting away the filth of the fpirit. That name into which all the faints are baptized is fuch, that their baptifm into it muft purify. Purification is the very thing itfelf, and that is the one plain reafon why it not only is, but muft be, a baptifm into the holy name: " for there is none other name under heaven given among men whereby we muft be faved,"

faved," Acts iv. 12. It is truly by the name, that we are faved; for this divine and living " name is as ointment poured forth," Cant. i. 3. This is the " unction from the holy one," 1 John ii. 20. " The name of the Lord is a strong tower; the righteous runneth into it; and is safe," Prov. xviii. 10. Well may they be safe in this name, seeing the baptifm into it is even faving.

Deeply fenfible that there was no other falvation, the Pfalmift prays, liv. 1, " fave me, O God, by thy name;" and, Jeremiah fays, x. 6, " thy name is great in might." Indeed this name is the ftrength and falvation of his people; none can run into his name, or be gathered into it, or baptized into it, but they muft at the fame time be gathered and baptized into him.—Hence the fcripture phrafe, " baptized into Chrift;" and hence alfo the abfolute certainty that where two or three are gathered into his name, there he is in the midft of them. See Mat. xviii. 20. He doth not fimply promife that he will be; he declares " there am I in the midft of them;" for he knew none could gather into his name, where he himfelf was not. The Greek word, truly tranflated, is into; the fame word ufed in Chrift's baptifmal commiffion, and with great propriety; for none can be gathered into him who are not baptized into him—neither gathering in his name, nor baptifm in it, profeffionally availeth. —The promife of falvation is fure to none but thofe who are truly gathered and baptized into the name itfelf: and to thefe it cannot fail; for the name has all healing virtue in it. " Holy Father" (fays Chrift) " keep through thine own name thofe whom thou haft given me, that they

may

may be one, as we are," John xvii. 11. " While I was with them in the world, I kept them in thy name," 12. If ye shall ask any thing" (says he) "in my name, I will do it," xiv. 14. This can never fail, any more than salvation can fail to such as are truly and thoroughly baptized into his name; for as this baptism is salvation, so asking in his name is in his own life, spirit and power, and he cannot deny himself. As the Father always hears him, because his asking in his the Father's life and power; so he always hears and cannot avoid hearing, all who ask in his name; for the one plain and all sufficient reason, that his name is his life and spirit, his power and presence; and all done in it, is done to purpose; for therein there is no lack—therein is fulness, and divine sufficiency. We are complete therein for ever, without any of the signs or symbols of former dispensations.

CHAP.

C H A P. VII.

Paul's epiftles to the Galatians and Coloſſians written purpoſely to diſſuade from attachment to ſhadowy ordinances. Circumciſion, water baptiſm, &c. plainly ſuperceded; and true Chriſtians ſhewn to be complete in Chriſt without them. This the evident ſcope of theſe epiſtles. This chapter contains many quotations from, and remarks on them.

SEVERAL of the epiftles feem to have been written on purpofe to diffuade from attachment to and retention of the rituals of fhadowy difpenfations. Paul having his knowledge of Chriſt by immediate revelation, knew the difpenfation of figurative inſtitutions was ended; and that Chriſtians viewing lifeleſs figns as gofpel ordinances, muſt powerfully divert and detain them from the living, faving fubſtance : hence he preffingly invites to Chriſt, the life and fubſtance, and warns againſt a continuance of ceremonials. —His epiſtles to the Galatians and Coloſſians, and a good deal of feveral others, are full to this purpoſe. Some troubleſome perſons had got in

among

among the Galatians, infifting on circumcifion, and the rites of the law; and had fo influenced the believers, that this infpired apoftle vehemently expoftulates with them for being fo eafily fhaken from grace (of itfelf fufficient for all) and turned to elementary obfervances, chap. i. 6, 7. " I marvel that ye are fo foon removed from him that called you into the grace of Chrift, unto another gofpel." But as rituals are not of the gofpel, he immediately adds, " which is not another; but there be fome that trouble you, and would pervert the gofpel of Chrift."—Indeed every attempt to eftablifh ceremonial inftitutions as gofpel ordinances, is directly an attempt to pervert the gofpel, and fruftrate its bleffed defign, that of fuperceding all thofe figurative obfervations. And on this ground he pronounces any one, even though it were himfelf and companions, or an angel from heaven, that fhould preach any other gofpel than that already preached unto them, accurfed, v. 18.—The gofpel that Paul preached, was Chrift within, the word nigh in the heart and in the mouth; which he exprefsly calls the righteoufnefs which is of faith; and declares of this inward word, " that is, the word of faith which we preach." See Rom. x. 6, 8.—A few words before he had declared, " Chrift is the end of the law, for righteoufnefs to every one that believeth." Hence it is evident, that this inward word of faith, which he preached as nigh in the heart, &c. is that which fupercedes and ends the figns and fhadows of the law to true believers.

The Ifraelites had a zeal of God, but not according to knowledge; for they being ignorant of God's righteoufnefs (the inward righteoufnefs of faith—Chrift, the word in the heart) and
going

going about to eftablifh their own righteoufnefs (in the figurative obfervances, the letter and cere- monies of the law, and creaturely performances) have not fubmitted themfelves unto the righte- oufnefs of God." See v. 2, 3. That he means by the righteoufnefs of God, this inward living word in the heart, and by their not fubmitting to it, their non-fubjection to the motions and teachings of it, is evident by the 6th, 7th and 8th verfes. " But the righteoufnefs which is of faith fpeaketh on this wife ; fay not in thine heart, who fhall afcend into heaven ? (that is, to bring Chrift down from above :) or who fhall defcend into the deep? (that is, to bring up Chrift again from the dead) but what faith it ? The word is nigh thee, even in thy mouth, and in thy heart; that is, the word of faith which we preach." This will remain, through all ages, the one only gofpel of life and falvation. It is Chrift in man, and ends the types and fhadows. Were it not Chrift himfelf the divine and holy word in the foul, did it not unite the life of the foul with the life of God, and bring into fubjection to him, dependence upon him, and action by him, it would never effect complete falvation for until all this is witneffed, God becomes not our " all in all." Though we have known Chrift after the flefh (faith the apoftle) yet now hence- forth know we him no more," 2 Cor. v. 16.—It was neceffary he went away, as to his vifible ap- pearance in the flefh, that he might come again, or more fully in fpirit abide with and comfort his for ever. This he promifed, and performs it to every true believer, who rightly looks for him in fpirit, not gazing up into heaven, watching for his outward coming, or feeking to know him after the flefh : unto all who thus inwardly look

for

for him, he appears in them, where his kingdom is " without fin to falvation." See Heb. ix. 28. This final coming to judgment will be to thoufands who look not for him, and will not be unto their falvation, but condemnation, to their fhame and everlafting contempt; but his fecond coming is promifed only unto them that look for him, and is to their falvation. And thus he did come to thofe he faid fhould not tafte of death till they faw the kingdom; for this is truly the coming of his kingdom on earth, to thofe who rightly wait and pray for it, and livingly experience it, which many then did; for fays the apoftle, Col. i. 13. " who hath delivered us from the power of darknefs, and hath tranflated us into the kingdom of his dear Son." Here Chrift fitteth on the throne of the heart, in his inward kingdom; for Paul tells the Galatians that it had pleafed God, who called him by his grace, " to reveal his Son in him," This entirely fupercedes the occafion of figns, as eating, drinking, or the like, to keep him in remembrance. This inward revelation and knowledge of the Son, in man, the hope of his glory, was a myftery that had been hidden from ages and generations.— The mifts of darknefs, and their refting in the law of carnal commandments and ceremonies, had hid and vailed from their minds the clear knowledge of it: but the vail being done away in Chrift to the faints, in that day, the apoftle declares this myftery was " made manifeft to them;" —and goes on to fhew what is the very life, riches and glory of it; faying, ".to whom God would make known what is the riches of the glory of this myftery among the Gentiles, which is Chrift in you the hope of glory." See Col. i. 26, 27.

There

There never was but one true life and fubftance
of religion.—Hence though this myftery of
Chrift within was greatly hid to moft men for
ages, yet was it the very thing Mofes referred
Ifrael to of old. Deut. xxx. 14, " the word is
very nigh unto thee, in thy mouth, and in thy
heart, that thou mayeft do it." Here Mofes
preached the gofpel: and Paul affirms it was
preached to Abraham, Gal. iii. 8. Indeed it
muft be fo; for Abraham faw Chrift's day, rejoiced in it, and came in degree into the life of
it, though not to the end of all the figns.—He
not only faw it, as then to come in greater fulnefs
and glory; he knew it in himfelf; for when the
Jews faid to Chrift, " thou art not yet fifty years
old, and haft thou feen Abraham?" he did not
efcape their delemma by telling them, Abraham
forefaw his day afar off. That was not the thing
he aimed at: but he came directly to the ever
important point, to the very life of the matter;
" verily, verily, I fay unto you, before Abraham was, I am," John viii. 57, 58: not I was;
for, as the holy word (the fame that appears in
the heart) he is the eternal *am*.—Abraham knew
and enjoyed him as fuch, as the life and fubftance
of the new covenant, " four hundred and thirty
years" before the giving of the outward law.—
This is the inward gofpel which Paul learned by
the revelation of Jefus Chrift, Gal. i. 12—by
God's revealing his Son in him: had he not fo
learned it, but only taken it by report from
others, though well authenticated, he might have
preached up Jefus and the refurrection in word,
with as much zeal as ever he had in the Jews religion, while he was fo " exceedingly zealous of
the traditions of his fathers," v. 14, and yet
.never

never at all have preached the gofpel of Chrift, which ever is in itfelf (and is never preached but in) the power of God to falvation.

I mourn that the preachers of our day fo generally lay hold of the hiftory of the gofpel in the letter, out of the life and power of it—zealoufly urging and ufing elementary obfervances, as ordinances of Chrift, to the fubverfion of many fouls from a clofe and fingle attention to the inward word of life; under which, for a feafon, they have been well exercifed. Thus "the letter killeth," 2 Cor. iii. 6. The literal preaching of what is called the gofpel, being out of the newnefs of life, leading into and landing in the ceremonials of religion, has flain its tens of thoufands, even of fuch as have in degree begun in the fpirit, and run well for a feafon; but by and by, through the influence of this lifelefs miniftry, have turned to and come under the fhadows, and there refted from the further purfuit of their journey in the fpirit, which they ought to have fervently profecuted in the open light, and under the warmth and animating beams of the fun. Paul knew the danger of thefe things, and confidered the attempts of thofe "falfe brethren" to continue the obfervance of outward ordinances, as directly tending to bring the believers "into bondage," Gal. ii. 4, and would not give place to them, "by fubjection" (to fuch obfervances) "no not for an hour, that the truth of the gofpel" (fays he) "might continue with you," v. 5. By the truth of the gofpel, he means its pure and genuine fimplicity, unfettered with figns and ceremonies; againft the retention whereof he was fo bold and faithful, that he declares

clares he even withstood Peter " to the face," at
Antioch, v. 11. and reproved him " before them
all," for compelling the " Gentiles to live as do
the Jews," 14; and especially, seeing he himself
had, " before that certain came from James,"
eaten with, and lived " after the manner of the
Gentiles."

AND then this great apostle pertinently inculcates, that even the believing Jews themselves
could not be " justified by the works of the law,
but by the faith of Jesus Christ," 16. It is evident he means, by the works of the law, the outward observances of it; for he is here expressly
labouring against the continuance of these, as
will yet further appear. The 3d chapter begins
thus, " O foolish Galatians, who hath bewitched
you, that ye should not obey the truth ?" the 2d
and 3d verses query, " this only would I learn
of you, received ye the spirit by the works of the
law, or by the hearing of faith? are ye so foolish?
having begun in the spirit, are ye now made perfect by the flesh?" all true religion, in every age
and nation, ever began in the spirit; and all that
ever continued in true religion, continued in the
spirit: and no man ever enjoyed any more of it
than he enjoyed in the spirit. None ever were, or
ever will be, " made perfect by the flesh;" by
any thing man, as man, can do; nor receive the
spirit by the works and observations of the law;
though many are acting as if they thought they
could not be complete in Christ alone, or be
" made perfect" in and by his holy spirit, without the addition of " weak and beggarly elements." It seems the Galatians were of the same

L   mind.

mind. They began in the fpirit, but not being content to abide in it, advance forward in it, and depend fingly upon it, they were feeking to be " made perfect," or completed in the work of religion, by ceremonial obfervations. Againft this departure from a fingle reliance on that holy fpirit which began the work, the apoftle was zealoufly engaged, and declares, v. 11. " the juft fhall live by faith." What faith? The righteoufnefs of that inward word of faith, which Paul preached " nigh in the heart and mouth." For there never was nor can be but one thing, through all time, that the juft could or ever can live by; and that is this inward word of life, the fpiritual flefh and blood of Chrift. " He that eateth me, even he fhall live by me," faith the bleffed Jefus, John vi. 57; and he that eateth him not truly and fubftantially (how oft foever he eats the figures, and how loud foever he pro- claims his faith) has " no life in him," 53. This is the tree of life, in the " midft of the paradife of God." This heals the nations of them that walk in the light of the lamb; and by this, and this only, they live unto God. Hence Paul fays, " I live, yet not I, but Chrift liveth in me; and the life which I now live in the flefh, I live by the faith of the Son of God." Gal. ii. 20; that is, by the faith of Chrift living in him. He was " dead to the law, that he might live unto God," 19. He renounces all mere legal, ceremonial righteoufnefs, and comes home to Chrift alive in his own foul. He mentions the " blefling of Abraham" as coming " on the Gentiles" only through " Jefus Chrift" the life; and the re- ceiving of " the promife of the fpirit," only
" through

" through faith," chap. iii. 14. This is experimental religion, all standing in that faith which is " of the operation of God" in the foul, Col. ii. 12. and which is the very life and " substance of things hoped for," and therefore, and therefore only, it is also the sure and certain " evidence of things not seen." See Heb. xi. 1. Many strive hard to believe, and think they do believe; but no mere opinion, or simple credence, is the faith of the gospel. No other faith than that which is in its own nature the very " substance of the things hoped for," can be a sure and unshaken evidence of the eternal inheritance, the things not yet seen.

" To Abraham and his seed were the promises made. He faith not, and to seeds, as of many; but as of one, and to thy seed, which is Christ. And this I say, that the covenant that was confirmed before of God in Christ, the law, which was four hundred and thirty years after, cannot disannul, that it should make the promise of none effect," Gal. iii. 16, 17. " And if ye be Christ's, then are ye Abraham's seed, and heirs according to the promise," 29. Observe, reader, the covenant is confirmed only in Christ, the life, the word in the heart, the inward " hope of glory." The promise is to all that are Christ's, and to them only, God promised that in Abraham, and in his seed, Christ, all nations should be blessed. This " promise is sure to all the seed;" see Rom. iv. 16; to all that are " born again of God," begotten into sonship and joint heirship with Christ, by this " incorruptible seed, and word of God," in the heart. This alone is the true faith, wherein all the children of it

L 2

" are

" are bleſſed with faithful Abraham," Gal. iii. 9.
It runs not in the outward blood, nor in the line
óf faith merely profeſſional. It was never obtained by the obſervance of rituals : nor is it
known but by a real baptiſm into death with
Chriſt, and ariſing with him in the newneſs of
life. " For if there had been a law given, which
could have given life, verily righteouſneſs ſhould
have been by the law," v. 21. But as nothing
can give divine life to the ſoul, but that which
brings it into the life of the ſon, or the ſtate of
real ſonſhip, by the union of the ſoul with the life
óf the holy word ; and as all thus begotten and
born of God, feel their dependence to be wholly
on God their Father; their looking is wholly
unto him for aid and protection. Hence this
great apoſtle, chap. iv. v. 6, of this epiſtle, de-
clarés, " becauſe ye are ſons, God hath ſent
forth the ſpirit of his ſon into your hearts, crying,
Abba, Father." Here is the alone true life of
faith in the ſoul. Here is divine reliance upon
the Father. It is in the ſtate of real ſonſhip, the
Emanuel ſtate, where God and man unite in the
heavenly fellowſhip, and ſubſtantial relationſhip.
This is beyond all figurative obſervations. " The
law made nothing perfect," but " was added becauſe of tranſgreſſions."—But for how long ?
" till the ſeed ſhould come, to whom the promiſe
was made," chap. iii. 19. But if the law was
added, becauſe of tranſgreſſions, till the ſeed
came, and John, the forerunner, to prepare his
way, declares the axe muſt be laid to the root of
the corrupt trees, till they are all " hewn down,
and caſt into the fire," and that the chaff muſt
be burned up, and the floor thoroughly cleanſed;
how idle is it, for any to think of ſalvation by
Chriſt,

Chrift, and that they are not under the law, but
under grace, becaufe they aſſent to the hiſtory of
the goſpel, and fay they believe in Jeſus, whilft
living a life of fin, and continuing in tranſgreſ-
fion, the very thing for which " the law was
added," and which the life, ſtrength and autho—
rity of the moral precepts of it were and will be
over, and therefore over men, fo far as in tranf-
greſſion, and fenfible of it; and fo far they are
and ever will be under the law, and not under
the dominion and government of grace. For
grace faveth; and juſt fo far as we are under it,
we are faved from fin; and fo far as we are not
faved from fin, we are not under grace. Chrift
never faves a foul in fin. Indeed, in the complete fenfe of the word falvation, he cannot. It
is a contradiction in itfelf. It would be faved,
and not faved. For falvation is from fin. Therefore it is faid, " thou fhalt call his name Jeſus"
(that is a faviour) " for he ſhall fave his people
from their fins," Mat. i. 21. The whole fcope of
the goſpel is falvation from fin, and a new life in
holineſs, really and inherently fo; not merely
imputatively. Mere imputation of Chrift's
righteoufneſs, without the implantation of it, is
a dangerous doctrine, indeed a real impoſſibility.
Chrift redeems from the ſhadows of the law, by
bringing and uniting the foul to the fubftance;
and that may be the main reafon why fo few pro-
feſſed Chriſtians are yet redeemed from them;
for none are any further truly redeemed, even
from the ſhadows, than they are fo by the life
and poſſeſſion of the fubftance. For as " circumcifion is nothing," fo fimple " uncircumcifion is
nothing." But the living faith, the new creature,
the fubftance, is all in all. Many think much

of

of themfelves, becaufe they are baptized in water, partake of the bread and wine, &c. And
many think much of themfelves becaufe they
avoid them, and fuppofe they fee beyond them.
But if even the latter is only a fpeculative or
merely rational convincement, it is nothing: it
is not the true and living redemption of Chrift
"from the rudiments of the world;" for that
never advances further or fafter in any foul, than
the foul advances in the knowledge and enjoyment of the fubftance. It is Chrift himfelf, the
feed, the life, the fubftance, that is the end of
the law. And fo, as none are truly redeemed
from the fhadows of it, but by and in the fubftance; fo none are redeemed from the curfe of
it, the penalty due for the tranfgreffions of its
moral precepts, until, nor a whit further than,
they know Chrift, the feed, the fubftance, to
finifh fin, and make an end of tranfgreffion in
them individually. For this is the only real deftruction of the works of the devil, that Chrift
ever makes; and confequently, all the redemption from the curfe, or penalty of the law, that
men ever really do know—fave the forgivenefs
and remiffion of fins already committed, through
the mercy of God in Chrift Jefus. So far, therefore, as we fin againft God, we are not under
grace, but at beft under the law. Nor fhall ever
"one jot, or one tittle, pafs from the law, till
all be fulfilled." If any foul is not under the
curfe of it, but under grace, it is becaufe Chrift,
the feed, redeems and preferves him from the
ftate of tranfgreffion, on account of which it was
added. And yet falvation is in no wife by the
deeds of the law, but by Chrift, who redeems,
and liveth in us, and is our life, above and beyond

yond the law. " Is the law; then, againſt the promiſes of God? God forbid," ſays the apoſtle, Gal. iii. 21. " But before faith came, we were kept under the law; ſhut up unto the faith which ſhould afterwards be revealed," 23. Before the word of faith is revealed in the heart, before the Son of God is revealed in men, as God revealed him in Paul, the law ſerves as a ſchool-maſter; hence the Apoſtle's very next words, verſe 24, are, " wherefore the law was our ſchool-maſter, to bring us unto Chriſt, that we might be juſti- fied by faith." Faith being the ſubſtance, as be- fore ſhewn, " of things hoped for;" and being " of the operation of God" in man, the word nigh in the heart, which is the word of faith the Apoſ- tles preached; when this was livingly known, in dominion over all in the ſoul, the uſe of the ſchool-maſter was ſuperceded: and this is the ſubſtantial experience of ſuch as are riſen with Chriſt, above the rudiments of the world, and the law of carnal commandments, in every age of the world. So the Apoſtle's next words are, v. 25, &c. " but after that faith is come, we are no longer under a ſchool-maſter. For ye are all the children of God, by faith in Chriſt Jeſus. For as many of you as have been baptized into Chriſt, have put on Chriſt." Here the law is fulfilled, in putting " on the Lord Jeſus Chriſt," —" the whole armour of light;" caſting "off the works of darkneſs," and making " no proviſion for the fleſh, to fulfil the luſts thereof," according to Rom. xiii. 12, 14. Well may this ſupercede the law, ſeeing this baptiſm into Chriſt, this put- ting him on, as the whole armour of light, ſo ef- fectually redeems from the works of darkneſs, and the luſts of the fleſh; agreeably alſo to Eph. vi. 11.

" put

" put on the whole armour of God, that ye may
be able to ftand againft the wiles of the devil."

SOME will underftand this baptifm into Chrift,
to mean outward baptifm. The author of the
aforefaid " plain account" quotes Bifhop Burnet,
defcribing the primitive baptifm in water, and
faying, " from whence came the phrafes of being
baptized into Chrift's death; of being buried with
him by baptifm into death; of our being rifen
with Chrift; and of our putting on the Lord
Jefus Chrift; of putting off the old man, and
putting on the new?" page 30. Thus men, by
attachment to rituals, are liable to have their
minds vailed, from beholding the obvioufly inward and fpiritual meaning of fcripture, or at
leaft turned to feek or fuppofe an outward fignification, where none feems neceffary or intended,
but that which centers in the life and fubftance.
Baptifm into Chrift, is into the name, the power
and influence of the divinity, according to the
commiffion. It is not true, that all who are baptized in water, " have put on Chrift;" but only
fuch as are actually baptized into Chrift himfelf,
the divine eternal fubftance; and therefore the
apoftle limits it to fuch only, by the words, " as
many of us." Thofe who hold water baptifm an
effential, or as that which faves, or is the " one
baptifm," I fuppofe, hold that all the believers
received it: but Paul fpeaks here of only as
many as were abfolutely baptized into Chrift, not
into water, verbally in his name, but into him,
fo as to put him on, by putting on his nature,
life and difpofition; love, meeknefs, temperance,
and all thofe virtues predominant in fuch in whom
he lives and reigns, and againft whom there is
therefore

therefore no law: for it is by thus putting on Chrift, and living in him, and he in us, our life, and hope of glory, in that wherein there is no tranfgreffion, that we are redeemed from the bondage, penalty and rudiments of the law, into " the glorious liberty of the fons of God." This is the one gofpel baptifm. It is ftrictly into Chrift, into the name, the faving name of the Lord, the ftrong tower of falvation and fafety, the name that is as ointment poured forth; the faving healing influences whereof make all the fincere virgins love him. The fame baptifm, with the fame word into, feveral times repeated, the apoftle again mentions, Rom. vi. 3. 4. "So many of us," and he might have faid only fo many, and doubtlefs meant fo, " as were baptized into Jefus Chrift, were baptized into his death. Therefore we are buried with him by baptifm into death. Now fee the fruits of it, which cannot refult from baptifm into water; "that like as Chrift was raifed up from the dead, by the glory of the father, even fo we alfo fhould walk in newnefs of life; and, verfe 5, " for if we have been planted together in the likenefs of his death" (that is, into a real death to all fin, for his baptifm thoroughly cleanfes the floor of the heart) " we fhall be alfo in the likenefs of his refurrection." This is what the apoftle means by walking in newnefs of life; as is plain by the connexion, " for if," &c. Can any thing be plainer, than that this is all an inward and fpiritual work; an actual baptifm into real death unto fin, and arifing into life with Chrift (that then liveth in us) in his inward refurrection and glory in the foul? and hence the baptifm that now faves us,

not

not the putting away the filth of the outward
flesh, but the anfwer of a good confcience towards
God, is rightly, and ever with divine propriety,
faid to be " by the refurrection of Jefus Chrift."
And now, to evince that this is all inward, and
that this of being " planted together in the
likenefs of his death," in baptifm, is not being
dipped into water, but into a real death to fin ;
let us obferve well, that the apoftle declares pofitively, without any exception, that if we have
been fo planted " into the likenefs of his death,
we fhall be alfo in the likenefs of his refurrection," which certainly is not true of all that are
baptized in water, though they may call that
" the likenefs of his death." For many have
been fo baptized, who have had no experience
of this likenefs of his refurrection, this walking
in newnefs of life. Simon the forcerer both believed (fee how little a mere lifelefs believing
amounts to) and was fo baptized; and yet he
was in the gall of bitternefs and bond of iniquity ; having neither part nor lot in the true
Chriftian baptifm, Acts viii. 13, 21, 23 : which
fhews plainly, that our bleffed Saviour's words
in the commiffion; Mark xvi. 16, " he that
believeth and is baptized fhall be faved," relate
wholly to that faith which is the fubftance of
things hoped for, and to that baptifm which is
truly into the likenefs of Chrift's death, into
death unto fin, and a new life unto holinefs, by
the refurrection and the life of Chrift in us, the
hope of glory. And as this in Mark, is the
fame commiffion with that in Matthew, it further
confirms that the baptifm mentioned in both is
that which is faving, and could not be that of
water ; fince the promife is to him that believeth,
and

and is baptized with it, that he "fhall be faved." This promife is fure, for this baptifm is
into the name of the Lord, the ftrong tower, in
which the righteous abiding, ever find fafety,
defence and prefervation; while a bare dipping
in water, profeffionally in the name, preferves
none from evil.

But further, that Paul meant as above explained, by this planting, death, burial and refurrection, his very next words declare, v. 6,
"knowing this, that our old man is crucified
with him, that the body of fin might be deftroyed,
that henceforth we fhould not ferve fin." This
is the death produced by the fiery baptifm of
Jefus, the crucifixion of our old corrupt man,
the deftruction of the body of fin in us. And is
it not ftrange, that any real Chriftian fhould not
underftand this, feeing it is the very thing which
John the Baptift (in direct contradiftinction to the
baptifm of water) declares of Chrift's, by the
mention of the axe, fan, and fire, and the work
effected by them, amounting to abfolute purification? May thefe things be well laid to heart,
by all who hope to be faved by a fimple though
hearty and fincere belief of facts, and immerfion
in outward water; for this is not the faith and the
baptifm to which the promife of falvation holds
good for ever. And for any to ufe water, as
gofpel baptifm, and not confider it faving, is to
run counter to the defign and exprefs declaration
of fcripture in regard to the baptifm of Jefus.

The fourth chapter to the Galatians begins af-
ferting, "that the heir, as long as he is a child,
differeth nothing from a fervant, though he be
lord

lord of all; but is under tutors and governors until the time appointed of the Father. Even so we, when we were children, were in bondage under the elements of the world," v. 1, 2, 3. Here we see the son himself submitted to the elements, the signs and ceremonials, unto which also the children were in bondage for a season; and to prevent their continuance under which, the apostle was now zealously endeavouring, having seen clearly beyond them himself, and been a living witness of their abolition. By the next verses, it is clear, that Christ's submitting to these elementary things, and being made under the law, was so far from perpetuating outward, elementary baptism, or any other rituals, that it was purposely " to redeem them that were under the law." Why then should we, who never were under that law of carnal ordinances, nor yet under the dispensation of John's baptism (which was for Christ's manifestation to Israel) unless by our own voluntary act, desire to come into bondage to these things, called here by Paul "the elements of the world?" Those outward things were abundantly proved weak and insufficient, or the law under which they were enforced had remained to enforce them still. All figurative immersions, sprinklings, eatings and drinkings, are altogether as weak, insufficient and unavailing, now, as ever they were; and it is an evidence of human weakness to continue in, and desire to be in bondage to them; as much so, as was the attachment of the Galatians to circumcision, &c. Paul, thoroughly convinced of this weakness of all mere signs and symbolical observations, therefore pertinently, and as it were with amazement, queries, v. 9, " how turn ye again to the weak

and

and beggarly elements, whereunto ye defire again to be in bondage?" 10, "Ye obferve days, and months, and times, and years." 11, "I am afraid of you, left I have beftowed upon you labour in vain." And how many days and times are now appointed, and rigidly obferved, even in our days? Set times and feafons, in man's will and wifdom, for fafting, prayers, thankfgivings, eating bread, and drinking wine, &c. And how much further a punctual conformity and obfervance, in thefe things, often goes towards conciliating the favour of men, and even of princes, than purity of life, integrity of conduct, and humanity towards all ranks of mankind, deferves ferious confideration. And is it at all ftrange, that Paul, obferving how great weight thefe weak things were obtaining, even among fuch as had really "known God," v. 9. (and who therefore had received that which was all-fufficient in itfelf, if lived in, and relied fingly on, for falvation, and eternal life, without any elementary obfervations whatever) was really alarmed, and afraid left his labours to eftablifh them in the purity and truth of the gofpel fhould prove in vain? efpecially when thofe who had lately almoft adored him, were fo foon and fo far infected with this zeal for ceremonials, as to give grounds for his query, v. 16, " am I become your enemy, becaufe I tell you the truth?" Is it ftrange, that he calls the retrograde motion of fuch as had "known God" for themfelves, from that inward knowledge, to outward rites, turning " again to the weak and beggarly elements?" In the next verfe, 17, fpeaking of thofe who ftrove to bring them into this bondage to the elements, he fays, " they zealoufly affect you, but not well; yea, they would

exclude

exclude you, that ye might affect them." They
were very zealous in their attempts to embondage
them to the elements, as too many now are; but
this zeal was not well, but very ill; for they
went so far, it seems, as to attempt or defire to
exclude such as were backward to conform, and
come into this bondage, that by this exclusion
they might be driven or prevailed on to affect
them, or their doctrines and notions. This their
zeal and labour was quite different from Paul's.
He was for the life; they, the letter. He for
the substance; they, the symbols. Do but hear
him, v. 19, " my little children, of whom I
travail in birth again, until Christ be formed in
you." He knew the letter killeth," and that
zeal in the sign often obstructs the growth and
formation of Christ, the substance in the soul: so
he travails as it were in birth again for their advancement and perfection in the latter. It would
seem, by their being truly his " little children,"
and by his now travailing in birth again, that is, for
the more complete growth and full formation of
Christ in them, that they had been already in degree truly begotten and born of God: and that the
Apostle, in the labour he had before bestowed
upon them, had already once travailed, as in
birth for and with them; but that they, instead
of rightly advancing in the travail, growth and
full formation of Christ in themselves, unto the
state of perfect men in him, " to the measure of
the stature of the fulness of Christ;" had been
obstructed and diverted therefrom, by turning to
the weak and beggarly elements;" and that therefore such was the Apostle's good will to them, he
was now again engaged in travail for their attain-
ment of what was lacking in them; the complete

formation

formation and growth of Chrift, whofe growth and increafe of ftature in man is gradual and pro-greffive: as was the cafe in that prepared body, wherein he grew, and "increafed in wifdom and ftature, and in favour with God and man," Luke ii. 52. And, to win them wholly to Chrift, and wean them from beggarly elements, Paul rea-fons with them in the following verfes, from Abraham's two fons, "the one by a bond-maid (repefenting this elementary bondage) the other by a free woman, Gal. iv. 22; the firft, " was born after the flefh," the laft, " by promife," 23: " which things" (faith he) " are an alle-gory; for thefe are the two covenants; the one from the Mount Sinai, which gendereth to bon-dage, which is Agar," 24. " For this Agar is Mount Sinai, in Arabia, and anfwereth to Jeru-falem, which now is, and is in bondage with her children," 25. " But Jerufalem, which is above, is free, which is the mother of us all," 26. And the few following verfes declare believers to be, with Ifaac, "Children of the promife;" that the children of the flefh perfecute thefe, as Ifh-mael did Ifaac; that the fon of the bond-woman was caft out, "for the fon of the bond-woman fhall not be heir with the fon of the free." And immediately upon thefe words the chapter con-cludes, "fo then, brethren, we are not children of the bond-woman, but of the free." And the next very pertinently begins, " ftand faft, there-fore, in the liberty wherewith Chrift hath made us free; and be not entangled again with the yoke of bondage." Then inftancing one par-ticular rite, he declares, " if ye be circumcifed, Chrift fhall profit you nothing;" that fuch as are fo, are debtors to do the whole law; that

Chrift

Chrift is become of no effect to thofe who feek to " be juftified by the law ; and pofitively af-ferts of them, " ye are are fallen from grace."

LITTLE do the zealous advocates for outward ordinances think how their attachment thereto hinders their real juftification, by the true and living faith and grace of the gofpel, even amidft all their talk of juftification, by faith in Chrift alone. Perhaps they never confider that thefe foolifh Galatians, with all their defires of bon-dage to the beggarly elements, might be as loud in profeffion of faith in Chrift, and in their claim to juftification by his blood, as any now are. I defire to know (if it is fo) why it is more im-poffible for a man circumcifed to be profited by Chrift, or why he is any more fallen from grace, than a man baptized in water. I cannot perceive that either circumcifion or baptifm prevents pro-fit by Chrift, any further than the mind is there-by turned from him, and from a fingle reliance upon the work of his grace in the heart for falva-tion ; nor that either the one or the other, or any other outward performance, will ever fail to prevent it, fo far as the mind is thereby turned away from an inward attention unto and firm dependence upon him who remains to be the refurrection and the life, in all true believers, the word nigh in the heart and mouth, for counfel, direction, and falvation. In fo far as any ceremonial diverts the mind of one that has truly " known God " in himfelf, from attention to his inward appearance and work in the heart, fuch an one is fo far " fallen from grace," and no further than he is fo diverted. And I can fee nothing in circumcifion a whit more likely fo to divert him, than in water bap-tifm,

tifm. One, as far as I can conceive, is juft as
likely to keep him from Chrift, as the other.
This may feem ftrange to many. But I think
they can give no found reafon why one fhould be
fo hurtful, and the other fo harmlefs, as they may
imagine. Diftinctions, however ill founded, when
long fettled in idea, feem real ; but examined to
the bottom, are found to have no exiftence but
in fpeculation. And believing many diftinctions
of long ftanding among Chriftian profeffors are
of this kind, I think I can truly fay, I travail in
fpirit, if not in birth, for them, that they may
dig deep for the foundation, and build on the
fure rock of ages. Then their buildings will not
fall, but ftand all winds and weathers. It is
much better patiently, with Paul (v. 5.) "through
the Spirit, to wait for the hope of righteoufnefs
by faith," than haftily to rufh into bondage, v. 7.
" Ye did run well ; who did hinder you, that ye
fhould not obey the truth ?" 8. . " This perfuafion cometh not of him that calleth you," 9. " A
little leaven leaveneth the whole lump." This I
firmly believe is juft the cafe with many, whom the
Lord in thefe days calls, by his holy Spirit working in them. They give up to the call ; begin,
like the Galatians, in the Spirit ; run well for a
feafon. By and by, in fteps the adverfary of
fouls, or, by the art and addrefs of fome high in
efteem with them, they are abfolutely hindered
from obeying the truth, in keeping fingly to the
Spirit they began in ; and by a perfuafion that
cometh not from him that called and ftill calleth
them to perfevere on in the Spirit, they are diverted to the elements, take up a falfe reft in the
fhadows, and gradually, perhaps almoft imper-
ceptibly to themfelves, depart from Chrift, the

M   inward

inward life; and fall away from the lively influences of grace in their own fouls, till the whole lump is leavened, with the leaven of the Pharifees; a fruitlefs, lifelefs zeal in rituals, a round of creaturely devotions and performances; drawing near the Lord with the mouth, and feeming to honour him with the lip, whilft the heart is far from him. In order to prevent which, I think Paul's direction, v. 25, very pertinent and proper: "if we live in the Spirit, let us alfo walk in the Spirit." And fo walking, I am perfuaded lifelefs forms will be forfaken, beggarly elements abandoned, old things done away, all things become new, all things of God, in fpirit and in truth, in the newnefs of divine life: for I can never believe, that the Spirit not only lived in, (as to what paffeth in the fecret of the foul) but alfo diligently and ftrictly walked in (as to all our outward religious or devotional exercifes) will fail to lead out of, or preferve from, every undue attachment to figns and ceremonials, or any thing that genders to bondage.

Now, notwithftanding the length of thefe quotations from the epiftle to the endangered Galatians, and of the foregoing remarks, I am not eafy to omit feveral paffages to the Coloffians; the epiftle to them alfo being pointedly againft fubjection to ordinances.

Paul was fervent in fpirit, in prayers and defires for them, that they might be "fruitful in every good work;" increafing in the knowledge of God, and "filled with the knowledge of his will, in all wifdom, and fpiritual underftanding,"

chap.

chap. i. 9, 10: but was fo far from pointing out water baptifm., or any other mere ceremonial, as promotive of this happy experience, as pertaining to fruitfulnefs in every good work, or as being included in the word every in this fentence, or at all belonging to thofe purely fpiritual things, wherein he wifhed them an increafed under-ftanding; that he plainly points out the fulnefs and fufficiency of Chrift, without them; and warns the Coloffians of their danger of being be-guiled with enticing words from the fimplicity of the gofpel. In leading on, and preparing their minds for a fingle dependence on Chrift alone, the living fubftance, and for the rejection of all that is not Chrift, nor in nor of his life in religion, he tells them it is he, v. 14, "in whom we have redemption:" that he is, v. 15, "the image of the invifible God;" yea, "the firft born of every creature." 16, That "by him were all things created that are in heaven, and that are in earth, vifible and invifible." 17, "And he is before all things, and by him all things confift." 18, That "he is the head of the body, the church:" that he is "the begin-. ning, the firft born from the dead; that in all things he might have the pre-eminence." And 19, that "it pleafed the Father, that in him fhould all fulnefs dwell." This was a good foundation; for having him actually living in us, in whom all fulnefs dwells, and he being truly our life, we need no addition of ceremo-nials. Therefore, the Apoftle, drawing on, v. 23, towards the fubftance, which he wifhes them to continue "grounded and fettled" in the faith of, not being "moved from the hope of the gofpel," he comes, 26, 27, 28, to the very

M 2   thing

thing itfelf; " the myftery which hath been
hid from ages and from generations, but now is
made manifeft to his faints: to whom God
would make known what is the riches of the
glory of this myftery among the Gentiles;"
which he exprefsly fays (as before noted) " is
Chrift in you, the hope of glory; whom we
preach, warning every man," &c.

Observe, reader, we before faw that " the
word of faith, which the Apoftles preached," was
the " word nigh in the mouth, and in the heart,"
as Paul plainly teftifies, Rom. x. 8. And here,
in full confirmation of the fame great truth, the
fame gofpel of falvation, we find the fame Apoftle
declares the Chrift, the gofpel, yea, the very
" riches of the glory of this myftery," of life and
falvation, " among the Gentiles," which they
the Apoftles preached, " is Chrift in you the
hope of glory." This is that " hope of the gofpel," which a few verfes before he wifhed they
might not be " moved away from." And to
keep them to this, and from ritual obfervances,
his labour was fervent among them, " ftriving
according " to the working of Chrift in him,
" which," (faith he, v. 29) " worketh in me
mightily." And this his fervent labour and
ftriving with them, preaching " Chrift in them "
as the fubftantial hope of glory, " warning every
man, and teaching every man, in all wifdom,"
was exprefsly in order, 28, to " prefent every
man perfect in Chrift Jefus;" where all perfection in the divine life centres; where God and
man are reconciled in the heavenly union; where
" he that is joined to the Lord is one fpirit;"
and figns are fuperceded. This was Paul's aim,
his

his fcope and exercife in this epiftle. In the beginning of the next chapter, he manifefts great
care or conflict for them, that " their hearts
might be comforted, being knit together in love,
and unto all riches of the full affurance of underftanding, to the acknowledgement of the myftery," (he had fpoken of) " of God, and of the
Father, and of Chrift; in whom " (fays he)
" are hid all the treafures of wifdom and knowledge." Thus he lays, or propofes, a fure foundation, on the all-fufficiency whereon both he
and they might fafely depend; and that without
aid or addition from things which may and muft
be fhaken, in order that that alone which cannot be fhaken may remain. For this alone is to
remain in the fulnefs of the gofpel ftate; and
furely no ceremonials are the things which cannot be fhaken. That this was Paul's aim, in
the foregoing expreffions, I think we have his
own authority to declare; for his next words are,
v. 4, "and this I fay, left any man fhould beguile you with enticing words." And v. 6, he
exhorts, " as ye have received Chrift Jefus the
Lord, fo walk in him." 7, " Rooted and built
up in him, and ftablifhed in the faith, as ye
have been taught, abounding therein with thankf-
giving." And then comes on pointedly to warn
them, and fhew them the danger of trufting or
being drawn away to any thing elfe but the
riches, glory and fufficiency of the great myftery,
wherein was all fulnefs for falvation : " beware"
(fays he, v. 8) " left any man fpoil you through
philofophy and vain deceit, after the tradition of
men, after the rudiments (in the margin, elements) of the world, and not after Chrift." Oh !
the mifchief of human philofophy, carnal reafon-

ings,

ings, vain deceit, and the wifdom of this world, in the things of religion. It builds tabernacles for abolifhed ordinances, and leads thoufands from Chrift to the rudiments of the world; thereby fpoiling them as to the increafe of knowledge and ftability in Chrift, who is all-fufficient for and in his people; as the next words emphatically declare, v. 9, 10, " for in him dwelleth all the fulnefs of the Godhead bodily. And ye are complete in him, which is the head of all principality and power." The next verfes fhew, that neither circumcifion nor outward baptifm is at all necefifary; fo entirely complete we are in Chrift, the inward and everlafting fulnefs and divine fufficiency. Do but read them. "In whom alfo ye are circumcifed, with the circumcifion made without hands, in putting off the body of the fins of the flefh, by the circumcifion of Chrift; buried with him in baptifm, wherein alfo ye are rifen with him, through the faith of the operation of God, who hath raifed him from the dead. And you being dead in your fins, and the uncircumcifion of your flefh, hath he quickened, together with him; having forgiven you all trefpaffes, blotting out the hand-writing of ordinances that was againft us, which was contrary to us, and took it out of the way, nailing it to his crofs." What could Chrift have done, or Paul have faid, more fully to have fhewn the abolition of ordinances? Even that of water baptifm is as plainly here expunged and fuperceded, as circumcifion. And it is marvellous to me, that men of fenfe, as the author of the forementioned " plain account," &c. with divers others, fhould be fo vailed in their underftandings, as to adduce this paffage, and feveral more of

somewhat

fomewhat a like import, in fupport of water baptifm ; when the manner of the Apoftle's bringing
it in, juft after warning them againft the rudiments of the world, pointing out the fulnefs of
Chrift, the inward hope of glory, and declaring
them complete in him, and then immediately
fhewing how they are complete in him, without
any of thofe rudiments he had juft warned them
againft, fhews as plainly as funfhine, that their
circumcifion and their baptifm were both in him,
the one as much as the other. So that I defire
the candid reader to turn to the paffage, and
read for himfelf. And I think he that can find
argument in it for water baptifm, may find as
much for circumcifion made with hands. But
as the circumcifion here is that made without
hands, fo alfo is the baptifm. It is all fpiritual : and, as the Apoftle words it, confifts "in
putting off the body of the fins of the flefh."
Almoft exactly fimilar is what he fays, Rom. vi.
6, fpeaking exprefsly of this inward and fpiritual
baptifm " into Chrift," and " into his death,"
being " buried with him by baptifm into death,"
&c. The words are, "knowing this, that our
old man is crucified with him ; that the body of
fin might be deftroyed, that henceforth we fhould
not ferve fin." Here the fame Apoftle afcribes
the fame effect to fpiritual baptifm into Chrift,
as in the paffage juft mentioned, in the epiftle to
the Coloffians, he afcribes to circumcifion fpiritually in him, the " putting off" or " deftroying the body of the fins of the flefh." It muft
be a wrong philofophy, and vain deceit indeed,
that can fo wreft thefe plain teftimonies of the
Apoftle, as to draw elementary water from them
for baptifm.

M 4   If

IF circumcifion here is inward, fo is the baptifm. If the baptifm is outward, fo is the circumcifion. They are fo joined together, that
neither true wifdom, found reafon, nor common
fenfe, can put them afunder, and make the one
outward, and the other inward. And if the
apoftle here excludes outward circumcifion, he
equally excludes outward baptifm. If he retains one, he retains both. But he retains neither. He clearly rejects both; and fhews our
circumcifion and our baptifm both complete in
Chrift, without hands, without a knife, or a fingle
drop of elementary water. He plainly fhews the
believers not only " buried with him in baptifm," but in the fame baptifm alfo " rifen with
him;" and that exprefsly " through the faith
of the operation of God;" which is wholly an
internal thing, the very " fubftance of things
hoped for." And having fhewn what the one
faving baptifm and circumcifion is, he then with
great pertinency exhibits Chrift " blotting out
the hand-writing of ordinances," taking " it out
of the way, nailing it to his crofs," as of no
further ufe to fuch as know him in the fellowfhip of his fufferings, and in the power of his
refurrection; fuch as experience his fulnefs, and
are circumcifed, baptized, and complete in him.
For thefe know his crofs, and are crucified by it
to the world, and to the rudiments, elements,
and ordinances of it; and the world alfo is crucified unto them. There is no friendfhip between Chrift and belial; nor much between his
difciples and the world. His religion does not
fuit the world. It is too fimple, unpopular, un-
pompous, and too unceremonious; too much a
death to felf. And I am well fatisfied that many,
who

who are and have been livingly wrought upon
by the power of God, and made to pant for divine fupport, have yet ftriven hard to fave their
life in felf, in popularity, and in the friendfhip
of this world; and from this difpofition have
fhunned the crofs; and though they have owned
Chrift, and chofe to be "called by his name, to
take away their reproach," they have ftill pre-
ferred to eat their own bread, and wear their
own apparel; and, with Nicodemus, to acknow-
ledge and worfhip the bleffed Jefus, in the dark
figns and fhadows of the night; than openly to
embrace the contempt of the crofs, and confefs
him in the inward, unceremonious purity, fpirituality and fimplicity of the clear and genuine
gofpel day. Dipping under water, and calling
that "buried with him by baptifm into death,"
the fpirit of the world, which ftill too much
liveth in them, can more eafily endure; nay, is
fometimes pleafed and plumed with it. Far be it
from me to think this of all who ufe this fign.
I doubt not, even this is a real crofs to fome;
but I believe it is generally much more tolerable
to the fpirit and wifdom of the world, than the
pure fimplicity of the gofpel; the real death and
burial with Chrift, in putting off the body of the
fins of the flefh, and ceafing from man, and from
their own creaturely activity in religion; waiting
on God, in abfolute dependence, in nothingnefs
of felf, and the lofs of all things: this is too hard
for the fpirit of the world. Thefe are hard fayings to it; who can bear them? Hence many
who walk with him awhile in the fpirit, and run
well for a feafon under the crofs, grow weary of
the fufferings and reproaches of Chrift, turn
away back, and walk no more with him; but

get

get into the "beggarly elements," and fit at
eafe in the friendfhip of the world, under a formal profeffion of religion; very little converfant
with the crofs, to which they would know all
thefe things nailed, if they rightly abode with
Jefus, and followed him in the regeneration.
But as none reign with him, but thofe who fuffer with him; as none rife with him in the likenefs of his refurrection, nor walk with him in
newnefs of life, but thofe who are really, not
ceremonially planted with him in the likenefs
of his death; as none fit with him in the throne
of his kingdom and glory, but who drink of his
cup, and are baprized with his baptifm; a rem-
nant of true-hearted followers have chofen to
fuffer affliction with him, and follow him, where
ever he leadeth, bearing his crofs. Thefe know
"the hand-writing of ordinances nailed to it."
Their blotting out, and removal, is a thing in
familiar experience with them; not merely a
matter of record in the letter of the fcriptures,
and thence gleaned up, and fyftemized into a
lifelefs creed, confeffion or profeffion of faith.

But let us follow the Apoftle a little further.
The next verfe fhews Chrift having "fpoiled
principalities and powers," and "openly tri-
umphing over them." Then he enjoins upon
the Coloffians, the way being now quite cleared
for it, "let no man therefore judge you in meat,
or in drink" (are not the bread and wine here
included, as we have feen circumcifion and elementary baptifm were a few verfes before?) "or
in refpect of an holy day, or of the new moon,
or of the fabbath day." He goes very thorough
in difmiffion of ceremonials, and well he might;
for his next words are, v. 17, "which are a
shadow

fhadow of things to come; but the body is of
Chrift." Therefore he adds, v. 18, &c. "let no
man beguile you of your reward, in a voluntary
humility, and worfhipping of angels, intruding
into thofe things, which he hath not feen; vainly
puffed up by his flefhly mind. And not holding
the head, from which all the body, by joints and
bands, having nourifhment miniftered and knit
together, increafeth with the increafe of God.
Wherefore, if ye be dead with Chrift from the
rudiments of the world, why, as though living
in the world, are ye fubject to ordinances?
Touch not, tafte not, handle not; which all are
to perifh with the ufing, after the commandments and doctrines of men." He does not fay,
wherefore, if ye be dead and buried with Chrift,
by plunging into the elements or rudiments in
water baptifm; but, quite differently, "wherefore, if ye be dead with Chrift from the rudiments," or, as the marginal reading has it, "from
the elements of the world, why, as though living
in the world, are ye fubject to ordinances?"
This home query fhould go to the heart of every
obferver of thefe outward ordinances, and beget
a clofe examination, whether their obfervance
thereof, and fubjection thereto, is not rather following after the traditions "and doctrines of
men," in their unfeafonable and unprofitable continuance in the abrogated inftitutions and ordinances of former difpenfations—the rudiments
which ought to be left behind, than after Chrift,
who has triumphed over them all, abolifhed, and
nailed them to his crofs? And when this examination is rightly made, and the Apoftle's pro-
hibitory injunction, "touch not, tafte not, handle
not, which all are to perifh with the ufing,"
&c.

&c. rightly complied with, I believe the "weak and beggarly elements" muſt be rejected ; bread, wine and water, as ordinances of religion, re-nounced, as things "which periſh with the uſing;" and the one only and ſaving baptiſm of the goſpel retained. Here the walking in newneſs of life, and the anſwer of a good conſcience towards God, by the reſurrection of Jeſus Chriſt, will be known. Here the earth will enjoy her ſabbaths - again, men reſting from their own works, as God did from his. Here the morning ſtars will ſing together, the ſons of God will ſhout aloud for joy, and the inhabitants of Sion keep holy day to the Lord.

C H A P.

C H A P. VIII.

Is a recapitulation or summary of a number of the principal reasons against supposing the Christian commission for baptism, Matt. xxviii. can mean water.

THUS having exhibited to the view of the reader many important passages of the sacred records, with many remarks and arguments thereon, which appear to me sufficient to satisfy the minds of such as may, under divine influence and illumination, carefully weigh and consider them, that the gospel is an inward, living and spiritual dispensation, void of any mere outward, figurative and ceremonial institutions, or ordinances; I think proper here, in one view, to recapitulate and present the reader with several of the principal arguments, or reasons, why the great gospel commission, Mat. xxviii. Mark xvi. cannot be properly understood to enjoin water baptism.

I. BECAUSE every religious washing in outward water, both under John and Moses, was symbolical of inward purification, and pointed to it, as effected " by the washing of regeneration, and renewing of the Holy Ghost." John's ministry, and water baptism, in particular, was for Christ's manifestation to Israel. To prepare his
way,

way, by turning their minds to fee the neceffity, and to a defire and readinefs for the reception of, and fubmiffion to, this his baptifmal purification; and then exprefsly to decreafe, as the fubftance fhould increafe. The type to give place to the antitype; feeing figns and fymbols were ever intended to vanifh out of the way, when the fubftance fignified by them was fully come: they being only as a fchoolmafter, to lead unto Chrift; who is, to every one that believeth in him, the full end of the law of commandments, contained in ordinances; becaufe they are complete in him, without any of thofe reprefentative obfervances, which only pointed at him, but can have no place in him, nor in his pure gofpel difpenfation.

II. Because the Greek word *en*, the common word for *in*, might have been ufed in the commiffion, as on other occafions, where *in* fimply was intended, if this baptifm had been only into water, verbally in the Lord's name. But the word *eis* being here ufed, fignifying directly *into*, and fo ufed in many other paffages, fhews the baptifm is into the name, the virtue, life and power of God; into holinefs, meeknefs, purity, gentlenefs, divine wifdom, true judgment, and whatever communicable grace or virtue a Chriftian receives by ingraftment into Chrift, when " cut out of the olive tree, which is wild by nature; and grafted, contrary to nature, into a good olive tree," as Rom. xi. 24. The ingraftment is plainly into Chrift. The baptifm is feveral times exprefsly declared to be into him. Nor need we doubt but the common word for teach, to wit, *didafko*, would have been ufed in
this

this commiſſion, had it not meant a converting, diſciplining, baptizing kind of teaching, which gathers ſouls into God, their habitation, refuge, and ſtrong tower.

III. BECAUSE the Apoſtles were not and could not be qualified to adminiſter this baptiſm, till they were endued with power from on high: could not impart, miniſter or communicate the Holy Ghoſt, but when and as they were baptized or filled with it themſelves. Hence were they commanded to tarry at Jeruſalem, till qualified by the outpouring of the Spirit upon them; and thus to wait for the promiſe of the Father, which they had heard of Chriſt, that " John baptized with water, but they ſhould be baptized with the Holy Ghoſt." And it is very abſurd to ſuppoſe Chriſt, in directing them how and where to wait, and what for, in order to their qualification to adminiſter his baptiſm, would expreſsly point their attention from and beyond that of water, to that of the Holy Ghoſt, had he been then giving them directions about preaching the goſpel, and baptizing in water.

IV. BECAUSE in all the after inſtances of baptiſm in water (through condeſcenſion) there is not one, wherein the form of words in this commiſſion is made uſe of; which it muſt have been in every inſtance, where the commiſſion was duly obſerved, had it meant water, and eſtabliſhed a form of words to be uſed in its adminiſtration. And how can we ſuppoſe thoſe, who now uſe water, better know, are more bound by, or more duly obſerve the commiſſion, than the diſciples? The diſciples were ſo far from underſtanding it

of

of water, that they never once ufed water, as under it; never once ufed the words of it, as a form in any wife proper to an outward or mere figurative performance. And does not this their total omiffion of thofe words evince that they were of an high and heavenly import, meaning nothing lefs than a real baptifm into the divine nature, the very life and fubftance of the God-head, and by no means applicable to the mere outward and vifible fign of this inward and fpiritual immerfion, ingraftment and purification? But men now prefume to apply thefe expreffions to a mere outward ceremony, and dignify immerfion in water, a moft unftable element, with the title of a gofpel ordinance; yea, a facrament of Chrift Jefus.

V. Because when the Holy Ghoft fell on Cornelius, and his houfhould, through Peter's fpeaking to them in the life and power of the fame, he was immediately made to remember (doubtlefs by the great and promifed remembrancer) the words of Chrift refpecting the baptifm of the Holy Ghoft. Thus clearly applying them to the falling of the Holy Ghoft on thofe Gentiles, through his miniftry; that is, through the words fpoken by him, whereby they fhould be faved, as foretold by the angel. And as only the baptifm of the Holy Ghoft is faving; as they did evidently receive this through Peter's miniftry; as the angel told Cornelius, Peter fhould tell him words by which they fhould be faved; and as Peter really underftood the baptifm they then received (through thofe words by him fpoken, and by which they were to be faved) to be the one faving baptifm of the gofpel, the very

fame

fame promifed by Chrift, in the words which
were thereupon brought to his remembrance; it
is evident the baptifm of Chrift is only inward.
And more efpecially, as at this very time, in regard to the baptifm of water, which was John's,
and was for Chrift's manifeftation to Ifrael, Peter
fo far doubted the propriety of its adminiftration
to the Gentiles, that he even appealed to the
judgment of men about it (which, how would he
have dared to have done, had it been his Lord's
command) and though none did forbid it, yet
he only commanded them to be baptized in the
name of the Lord (the Greek word here is *en*)
and not into the name of the Father, and of the
Son, and of the Holy Ghoft; thefe words in no
wife fuiting the nature and defign of that outward adminiftration.

VI. BECAUSE Peter not only never baptized any
in water afterwards, that we have any account
of, but exprefsly declares the faving baptifm;
both negatively, what it is not, to wit, "putting
away the filth of the flefh," the proper effect of
water; and pofitively, what it is, and by what it
is effected; it effects, in its complete operation,
fuch a thorough purification, as eftablifhes in the
foul, the anfwer of a good confcience towards
God, and is effected by that which only can do
this, the "refurrection of Jefus Chrift," the
light, and life, and hope of glory in us. And
it will for ever be in vain for any to fuppofe they
have received Chriftian baptifm, unlefs they thus
know him to be truly and experimentally " the
refurrection and the life " in themfelves; for
this alone can produce the true fanctification and
baptifm of the gofpel. A figure cannot fave us.

All the wafhings in water are figures. And one
figure is not the fign of another figure. Neither
any of the divers Mofaic wafhings, nor John's
immerfion (being all but figures) pointed to the
baptifm of the gofpel, as to an outward figurative plunging in water; but as (which in truth
it is) to an inward, fpiritual wafhing, in the
true laver of regeneration. And I think the old
Mofaic typical laver might be as properly continued under the gofpel, as fprinkling or dipping
in water.

VII. BECAUSE Paul, a moft eminent Apoftle,
not a whit behind the chiefeft, and who received
his commiffion and his knowledge of Chrift by
immediate revelation (God revealing his Son in
him) and thereby knew his will, and the true
fpiritual nature of his baptifm; fpeaking of that
with water, declares pofitively, that "Chrift fent
him not to baptize, but to preach the gofpel;"
and even thanks God he had baptized no more;
which would have been an high prefumption, and
mifdemeanour, had he not known that baptifm in
water, was no more an ordinance of Chrift, than
circumcifion made with hands. But knowing the
circumcifion, and baptifm of the new covenant,
were altogether inward, he fays, writing to the
Coloffians, "ye are complete in him, which is
the head of all principality and power; in whom
alfo ye are circumcifed with the circumcifion
made without hands, in putting off the body of
the fins of the flefh, by the circumcifion of Chrift;
buried with him in baptifm, wherein alfo ye are
rifen with him, through the faith of the operation
of God, who hath raifed him from the dead, chap.
ii. 10, 11, 12: thus plainly rejecting both outward

ward circumcifion and baptifm, the one as much
as the other; and fhewing that the inward,
wherein they are complete in Chrift, is a real
putting off the body of fin, a death unto it, a real
burial with Chrift, and rifing with him; which
is fo far from dipping under and rifing out of
the water, that it is only by a faith that is fo
living, and fo much above all that is outward,
and merely of man, that it is truly and powerfully of the very operation of God in the foul.
Here is that refurrection of Chrift, by which the
good confcience is witneffed in Chriftian baptifm. And having thus fhewn believers' baptifm
to be as entirely inward as their circumcifion,
he immediately and very pertinently reminds
them of Chrift's " blotting out the hand-writing
of ordinances," and taking " it out of the way,
nailing it to his crofs;" cautions them to let no
man judge them in refpect to thofe outward
things, which are but "a fhadow of things to
come," and then roundly queries of them,
"wherefore, if ye be dead with Chrift, from the
rudiments or elements of the world, why, as
though living in the world, are you fubject to
ordinances?" This fhews, " dead with Chrift,"
or planted in the likenefs of his death, is not
a burial into the rudiments, or elements, as in
outward baptifm, but " dead with Chrift, from
the rudiments;" therefore he immediately enjoins, "touch not, tafte not, handle not, which
all are to perifh with the ufing, after the commandments and doctrines of men." By all which
we not only perceive his full rejection of all the
mere fhadowy ordinances, but that he was fo far
from efteeming water baptifm to be Chrift's, that
he was truly, thankful to God that he had never

N 2   ufed

used it, even in condescension, but in a very few instances; and that he considered the real baptism into Christ to include a death with him from all those rudimentary or elementary things which perish with the using; and which, therefore, are not to be touched, tasted, or even handled, as ordinances, nor by any means subjected to, by those who are dead to them by baptism into death with Christ.

VIII. Because all those who truly believe, and in this faith of the operation of God are baptized according to the commission, are thereby saved, as promised by Christ, in giving the commission; which is not true of all who are baptized in water. Simon the sorcerer both believed and was baptized; and yet, at the same time, was so far from having any lot, part or portion in gospel faith or baptism, that he was in the very "gall of bitterness, and bond of iniquity;" which no doubt has been the case with too many beside Simon: whereas all who are baptized according to the commission, and therein witness the floor of the heart thoroughly cleansed, are baptized into Christ, have put him on, the "whole armour of light," and thus being planted in the likeness of his death, are alive in the likeness of his resurrection, in true newness of life.

IX. Because we have no account, nor the least reason to believe, the first Apostles were ever baptized in water, after John baptized them; for "Jesus himself baptized not." And we have heard of none else authorized to baptize them therein, but John; and so they being outwardly baptized only into John's baptism, if Christ's was
also

alfo outward, and John's was not it, they never
had it. And then they would have been fent to
baptize others with a baptifm themfelves never
received. But they received freely, and were
freely to give, and could not give what they
never received, nor what they did receive, before
they had received it: and therefore were under
an abfolute neceffity to wait till they actually did
receive the baptifm of the Holy Ghoft, before
they poffibly could baptize others with it. This
they did receive, and this they did adminifter;
and their not prefuming, nor being allowed by
their Lord, to attempt baptizing according to
the commiffion, till firft thus baptized themfelves, fhews evidently what the baptifm of the
commiffion was, and that the qualification for
its adminiftration was through the fame baptifm
firft received in themfelves, the endument of
power from on high. But had the commiffion
intended John's baptifm, that they were qualified
to adminifter, and did adminifter before; had it
intended water, and yet not as John's, they never receiving it after the commiffion, any more
than before, were no more qualified to adminifter
it afterwards, than before. Hence it refults, that
Chrift's is that they waited for, received, and
then, through the communications of it, adminiftered to others; that is, the one baptifm of
the gofpel.

X. Because whoever receive Chrift's baptifm,
are initiated thereby into the church of the firft-
born, the pillar and ground of truth, and have
their names written in heaven, have the white
ftone, and new name: and being buried, and
rifing with Chrift, are joint heirs with him; and
he is not afhamed to call them brethren, they in
all

all things reverently afcribing to him the pre-eminence. But this is by no means true of all that
are baptized into water. This is in fubftance
fomewhat the fame as the 8th reafon; but may
ferve to fhew, that as baptifm in water is not
faving, fo it never initiates any into the church
of Chrift, however it is extolled as an initiatory
ordinance.

XI. Because Chrift himfelf, though he was
circumcifed, baptized, &c. outwardly, in order
to fulfil, terminate, blot out, and for ever difan-
nul all fuch ceremonials, never circumcifed or
baptized others outwardly; nor ever ordered any
of the multitudes that believed on him, that we
have any account of, to receive either. He even
wafhed his difciples' feet, and taught them to
wafh one another's; but never baptized them in
water, which we may venture to believe he would
by no means have omitted, had it been his own
baptifm, the one faving and perpetual baptifm of
all true believers.

XII. Because he did baptize them with the
holy Spirit, declaring he fent them even as his
Father fent him; that is, anointed with the Holy
Ghoft, that they fhould do the works which he
did (baptize with the Holy Ghoft, before, was
a work which he did.) And as, in order to qualify them, he breathed on them, and bid them
receive the Holy Ghoft, this was truly fending
them as he was fent, and turning their minds,
and fixing their dependence, on the like anointing, for qualification for the like fervices.

XIII. Because baptifm in water is certainly
one

one of the old things, one of the things that can
be fhaken; and not one that remains, when and
where all are fhaken and removed, that can be
fhaken; not one that can remain, when and
where not only the earth, not only fin, carnality,
and earthly mindednefs, but alfo heaven; things
efteemed heavenly, and which were once really
ordinances of God, are thoroughly fhaken, and
all removed, but what cannot be fhaken; and
which alone can remain in this truly gofpel ftate.
The rejoicing of true Chriftians is in that which
God creates, after the old heavens and old earth
are fhaken, and all typical righteoufnefs is paffed
away; that is, in the pure antitypical righteoufnefs which muft remain, becaufe it cannot be
fhaken, but is of the very nature of, and per-
taineth to the new heavens, and new earth, wherein dwelleth righteoufnefs, in its pure, uncum-
bered, unceremonious fimplicity and beauty. The
elements (thefe elementary, figurative obfervations) are known, in the truly gofpel ftate, to
melt with fervent gofpel heat; whilft too many
are retaining thefe, and expecting the outward material elements to be melted with outward material
fire, at the end of this outward material world.
Thus miffing the marrow and fubftance of things,
through the outwardnefs of their ideas and expectations.

XIV. Because it is certain, that it does pleafe
God to fave fome through the foolifhnefs of
preaching, to wit, fuch as truly believe. No
foul can be faved, but according to God's mercy
"by the wafhing of regeneration, and renewing
of the Holy Ghoft." This is Chrift's baptifm.
And hence it follows, that every foul faved
through

through preaching, muft thereby be baptized
with the Holy Ghoft and fire, or witnefs the re-
generating wafhing, and renewal of the Holy
Ghoft. For this being that without which none
can be faved, it is idle to think of preaching,
faving, or contributing towards the falvation of
any, but through the work of this baptifm.
If preaching at any time contributes more or lefs
to falvation, it certainly contributes in the fame
degree to this fpiritual baptifm. Thus Paul
begat fouls to God through the gofpel. But no
miniftry that is not baptizing, can ever do this.
And this' is the reafon why they who run without God's fending and qualification, do not
profit the people. They cannot baptize them
into the name by all their arts of rhetoric, and
powers of elocution. That is a work furpaffing
the utmoft influence of all fuch unauthorized miniftry, and effected inftrumentally, by no other
preaching than that which has its efficacy from
the power received from on high. This even
the Apoftles were under an abfolute neceffity to
wait for, and receive too, before they could thus
teach baptizing. And the fame neceffity of waiting for the fame qualification will remain, to
all Chrift's true miniflers, to the world's end.
Indeed the fubftance of the injunction, tarry at
Jerufalem till you are endued, &c. refts now
with equal force on all who are equally obfervant of divine direction, in the work of the
gofpel. And to thefe Chrift's words for ever
hold good, " he that receiveth you, receiveth
me; and he that receiveth me, receiveth him
that fent me." Mat. x. 40. They who truly receive Chrift, receive his baptifm. Hence none
truly receive his minifters, and their miniftry,
but

but therein and therethrough they receive him and his baptifm. This muft hold good for ever; they who truly receive him, know it. It would be as true, if it had never been fo expreffed. Experience would livingly confirm it. But they rejoice that this great truth is fo clearly, and by fo many modes of expreffion, eftablifhed in the facred records. And their prayers are fincerely and fervently to God, that feeking fouls may be enabled to fee, hear and believe it, to the falvation of their fouls, in the faving operations of the one only foul-faving baptifm of Jefus.

F I N I S.

BOOKS publiſhed by J. PHILLIPS,

George-Yard, Lombard-Street.

No Croſs, No Crown: A Diſcourſe, ſhewing the Nature and Diſcipline of the Croſs of Chriſt, &c. By W. Penn. 8vo. New edition bound 5s.

Ditto in French, a new Tranſlation, 6s. bound.

Fruits of Solitude, in Reflections and Maxims, relating to the Conduct of Human Life. By William Penn. A neat Pocket Volume. Price 2s. 6d.—Ditto in French 2s. 6d. calf and lettered.

Fruits of a Father's Love: being the Advice of Wm. Penn to his Children, relating to their Civil and Religious Conduct. 6d.

Miſcellanies Moral and Inſtructive, in Proſe and Verſe; collected from various Authors, for the Uſe of Schools, &c. A new Edition, with Additions. Two Vols. Price 5s. Each Volume may be had ſeparate.

The Power of Religion on the Mind, in Retirement, Affliction, and at the Approach of Death, &c. The ſixth Edition, corrected and much enlarged. Price 2s. bound.

Piety Promoted, in Brief Memorials of the virtuous Lives, Services, and Dying Sayings, of ſome of the People called Quakers, formerly publiſhed in Eight Parts. By John Tomkins and others; now reviſed by John Kendall, and placed in the order of time. A new edition, 3 vols. 9s. 6d. ſheep rolled, and 10s 6d.

Medical Botany, containing ſyſtematic and general Deſcriptions, with Plates, of all the Medical Plants, Indigenous and Exotic, comprehended in the Catalogues of the Materia Medica, as publiſhed by the Royal Colleges of Phyſicians of London and Edinburgh, &c. By W. Woodville, M. D. 3 Vols. in Boards—Plain 2l. 5s.—Coloured 5l. 8. Now publiſhing in Weekly Numberss Part Second of Medical Botany, containing Deſcription, and Plates of the Medicinal Plants in the foreign Pharmacopeias. Price 1s. plain—coloured 2s. 6s.

Return of the whole Number of Perſons within the ſeveral Diſtricts of the United States, &c. Price 1s. 6d.

An Account of the Sugar. Maple Tree of the United States, and of the Methods of obtaining Sugar from it, &c. By B. Ruſh, M. D. Price 4d.

On

On the Punifhment of Murder by Death. By B. Rufh, M. D. Price 6d.

An Effay on the Nature and Conftitution of Man; comprehending an Anfwer to the following Queftion, propofed by a learned Society:—"Are there any fatif-" factory proofs of the immateriality of the Soul: if fuch " Proofs exift, what conclufions are to be formed from " them with refpect to the Soul's Duration, Senfation, " and Employment, in its State of Separation from the " Body?" By R. C. Sims, M. D. Price 2s.

Juſt publiſhed,

Some Account of the Life and Religious Labours of Sarah Grubb. Second Edition.

Sacred Hiftory; or the Hiftorical Part of the Holy Scriptures of the Old and New Teftaments, digefted into due Method, with refpect to Order of Time and Place. With Obfervations, tending to illuftrate fome Paffages therein. By Thomas Ellwood. In 3 large Vols. 12mo. Price to Subfcribers 10s 6d well bound, or 12s Calf lettered, delivered in London. The Price will be advanced to Non-Subfcribers.

Printing by Subfcription.

The Hiftory of the People called Quakers; by Wm. Sewell. The Price to Subfcribers will be 12s. bound in Calf and lettered. To Non-fubfcribers 15s.

Samuel Bownas's Life, in one Volume 12mo. Price to Subfcribers 2s. Sheep. To Non-fubfcribers 2s. 6d.

John Gratton's Life, in one Volume 12mo. Price to Subfcribers 1s. 6d. in Sheep. To Non-fubfcribers 2s.

Richard Davies's Life, in one Volume 12mo. Price to Subfcribers 1s. 3d. in Sheep. To Non-fubfcribers 1s. 6d.

www.ingramcontent.com/pod-product-compliance
Lightning Source LLC
Chambersburg PA
CBHW020626030726
47497CB00007B/2436